W9-BST-924

HUMBOLDT COUNTY

Detail area

CALIFORNIA

TRINITY COUNTY

Redcrest

Eel River

Weott

AVENUE OF THE GIANTS

Myers Flat

Salmon Creek

Miranda

SALMON CREEK

Eel River

Phillipsville

South Fork Eel River

Alderpoint

Briceland

Redway

Garberville

Harris

WHITETHORN JUNCTION

Benbow

Whitethorn

RICHARDSON GROVE STATE PARK

MENDOCINO COUNTY

101

Whale Gulch

HUMBOLDT

Life on America's Marijuana Frontier

EMILY BRADY

GRAND CENTRAL
PUBLISHING

NEW YORK   BOSTON

Grand Central Publishing
Hachette Book Group
237 Park Avenue
New York, NY 10017

www.HachetteBookGroup.com

Book design by Carin Dow
Printed in the United States of America

RRD-C

First Edition: June 2013
10 9 8 7 6 5 4 3 2 1

Grand Central Publishing is a division of Hachette Book Group, Inc. The Grand Central Publishing name and logo is a trademark of Hachette Book Group, Inc.

The Hachette Speakers Bureau provides a wide range of authors for speaking events. To find out more, go to www.hachettespeakersbureau.com or call (866) 376-6591.

The publisher is not responsible for websites (or their content) that are not owned by the publisher.

Library of Congress Control Number: 2013932822

For my grandmother,
Alice Brady,
who encouraged me to go out into the world,
and to write about what I found there.

To live outside the law,
you must be honest.
—Bob Dylan

CONTENTS

Author's Note   ix

Glossary   x

PROLOGUE   1

CHAPTER ONE — Mare   3

CHAPTER TWO — Crockett   16

CHAPTER THREE — Emma   34

CHAPTER FOUR — Bob   47

CHAPTER FIVE — Mare   58

CHAPTER SIX — Emma   74

CHAPTER SEVEN — Bob   90

CHAPTER EIGHT — Crockett   105

CHAPTER NINE — Mare   116

CHAPTER TEN — Emma   126

CHAPTER ELEVEN — Bob   139

CHAPTER TWELVE — Mare   151

CONTENTS

CHAPTER THIRTEEN — Emma   164

CHAPTER FOURTEEN — Bob   170

CHAPTER FIFTEEN — The Vote   178

CHAPTER SIXTEEN — Bob   195

CHAPTER SEVENTEEN — Emma   205

CHAPTER EIGHTEEN — Crockett   216

CHAPTER NINETEEN — Mare   227

Author's Remarks   241

Acknowledgments   247

Index   251

AUTHOR'S NOTE

This book is narrative nonfiction. The characters are real and the events happened. Passages expressing a person's thoughts or feelings have been fact-checked. Because the cultivation of marijuana remains a federal felony, despite state law, punishable by a sentence of up to life in prison, the names and certain identifying characteristics of some of the people in this book have been changed.

A LITTLE HUMBOLDT GLOSSARY

215: Proposition 215, California's 1996 medical marijuana law. Also, shorthand term for the doctor's recommendation that allows one to use or grow marijuana for medicinal purposes.

Back-to-the-Land: A migration movement from cities to rural areas by American youth that began in the late 1960s.

Bank of the Woods: Cash savings that are buried or hidden on one's property, often in plastic tubes, glass jars, or recycled pickle or pepperoncini barrels.

CAMP: The Campaign Against Marijuana Planting. A multi-agency task force created in 1983 with the goal of eradicating marijuana cultivation throughout California.

CAMP'ed: A verb used by pot growers to describe a garden that has been destroyed or confiscated by law enforcement.

Cartels: Criminal organizations blamed by law enforcement for massive grows found on public land, despite lack of evidence linking them to Mexican organized crime.

Depping: Light deprivation; an agricultural technique of covering outdoor pot plants with a black tarp to simulate nightfall and induce flowering and an early harvest.

Diesel dope: Marijuana grown under lights powered by diesel-powered generators.

Fronting: Providing pot to a dealer on condition that you will be paid once the dealer sells it to someone else.

Guerrilla growing: Growing pot on someone else's land or public land without permission. More common among small growers before medical marijuana; now largely attributed to cartels.

Grow or Scene: A marijuana garden.

Grower: Someone who grows pot; could be six plants or six hundred.

Hempheimers: Marijuana-induced forgetfulness.

Hipneck: A hippie-redneck hybrid. Such a person might be named Sunshine, drive a big truck, and grow a lot of marijuana.

Homestead: A home built by its owner, often located off the electrical grid with no indoor plumbing and with a small marijuana patch growing out back next to the vegetable garden.

Humboldt time: A relaxed notion of time; the opposite of punctual.

Humboldt twenty: A hundred-dollar bill.

Marijuanaries: Places envisioned for some time in the future where tourists can visit and sample pot and learn about how it is grown and harvested.

Pot Princess: An attractive young woman who dates wealthy growers who have giant trucks and gardens. Also known by the more negative term "potstitute."

Prologue

Follow the same path as the youth who once fled the city. From San Francisco, cross the Golden Gate and head north through the rolling hills of Marin, and then Sonoma County. Keep going. In the summertime, the landscape is a sun-scorched ocher. After the rains have begun, it is an Irish shade of green. Continue through the vineyards to Mendocino. Hours will pass. The grassy hills give way to ragged mountains, and the trees grow pointy and thick. On foggy days, the treetops catch the mist that billows in off the Pacific, and clumps of it hang there like fallen clouds.

Past the South Fork of the Eel River the road winds through a patch of ancient redwood forest called Richardson Grove State Park. These trees, the coast redwoods, are the tallest living things on earth. They come from another time; their ancestors provided shade for dinosaurs. California's redwood forest once stretched from the Oregon border south to Big Sur. Then, in the 1850s, men who came west seeking adventure and riches discovered the beauty and durability of the wood. They called it red gold. Trees were leveled. Fortunes were made. Today, only 4 percent of California's old-growth redwood forest remains, like a magnificent cathedral that has been knocked to the ground, with only its gilded altar left standing.

In Richardson Grove, the redwoods loom mere inches from the roadway, and the trunks of the larger ones may be wider than your car. The oldest tree in the grove is called the Grandfather. Shaped like a giant slingshot, with two trees sprouting from his base, the Grandfather is about twenty-four stories high and has stood for more than 1,800 years. His rings tell the story. Just beneath the fibrous bark, man landed on the moon. Deeper inside, Columbus sailed across the Atlantic. Toward the core, Mayans were beginning to carve their language into temple walls.

Inside the grove, even on a warm summer day, it is dark and cool. Most of the sunlight is caught in the branches of the giants high above, but in places, it filters down, leaving delicate lacelike patterns on the road.

Keep driving. You're almost there. Richardson Grove marks the unofficial entrance to Humboldt County. Pass through it and you'll begin to understand the local saying about living in a world that exists behind the redwood curtain.

CHAPTER ONE

Mare

Late one Tuesday afternoon in March of 2010, in a disorderly cabin located on the edge of the North American continent, in a place bypassed by highways and the electrical grid, Mary Em Abidon reached deep into her freezer, plucked out a small white marrowbone, and tossed it onto her pantry floor. Her dog, Lucky, was nearly deaf, but the unmistakable *thunk* of bone hitting wood could still roust him from his slumber. It was a familiar routine between Mare, as she was known to most everyone, and the border collie/cocker spaniel mutt she found abandoned on the road to Shelter Cove fourteen years earlier.

As Mare bent down to scratch behind Lucky's floppy black ears and pat his head, the little dog peered up at her with pleading eyes.

"Lucky, stay and guard," she instructed him, as she always did before she left for town.

Lucky picked up his treat and headed for the front deck

to curl up under the cherry trees that were just beginning to bud, while Mare gathered up her coat and purse and pulled the cabin door shut behind her. She was excited, giddy even, as she started up her battered Volvo station wagon and eased it down her driveway and toward town. It was the same fluttery feeling she had long ago when she first moved to this place. It felt like the start of something new.

Mare had first heard about the event while listening to KMUD-FM, the community radio station. A local talk show host named Anna "Banana" Hamilton was organizing it. The flyers she posted around town advertised the event two ways: "The Post-Marijuana Prohibition Economy Forum," and the shorthand version, which rolled off the tongue much easier: "What's After Pot?" The accompanying art featured a pot leaf, two nude female figures wearing baseball caps, clumps of trimmed marijuana buds, and what appeared to be dollar bills with wings fluttering away. Smaller print near the bottom of the flyer advised attendees to bring their own snacks.

On her way to town, Mare caught slivers of the steel-blue Pacific Ocean through the trees, but mostly all she could see were the trees themselves. On her right, madrones and Douglas firs plunged down the canyon. On her left, they furrowed their roots deep into the hillside. The Volvo rattled past a row of brightly painted mailboxes and the dirt road that led to the meadow where the annual Easter egg hunt and the May and October trade fairs were held. Farther ahead was the tiny community school where years earlier Mare had volunteered as an art teacher, teaching the children how to make paper and pinch clay into faces that they would stick to trees until the rain washed them away.

At the intersection called Four Corners, where a hand-painted blue sign cautioned drivers to be on the lookout for bicycles, motorcycles, a donkey, and children, Mare guided the Volvo past the entrance to Sinkyone Wilderness State Park, and onto a road that straddled the Mendocino and Humboldt county line. Deep inside the state park was a seventy-five-acre patch of ancient redwoods that Mare had once fought to save from the roar of a lumber company's saw. Looking back on her life, Mare considered it the most important thing she'd ever done.

That was nearly thirty years ago. On this March day, Mare was a month into her seventieth year. Her once-blond hair had long since turned silvery white, and her handsome face carried the lines of a life fully lived. Her blue eyes still twinkled with unfaltering optimism, and she continued to marvel at the details, like the cherry-red paint on a passing motorcycle, which could make her exclaim in childlike delight. But her body had begun to betray her. Her right knee caused her to hobble, and she had had to have a hip replaced a few years back. "Becoming bionic," she called it. Her sturdy, creative hands, which once made a thousand ceramic pots a year, were now racked with arthritis. They gripped the Volvo's steering wheel and propelled her toward town.

The meeting was taking place at the Mateel Community Center in Southern Humboldt, an area of 1,200 square miles of sprawling wilderness in the far reaches of Northern California. The area used to be known as the Mateel, after the Mattole and Eel rivers that flow through it, but now, as if it were some Manhattan neighborhood, many people called it by the abbreviated term SoHum.

Over the years, SoHum, the rest of Humboldt, and neighboring Mendocino and Trinity counties had become known around the country as the Emerald Triangle, after the region's brilliant green clandestine marijuana crop. Since the mid-1970s, outlaw farmers throughout the Triangle had been supplying America with its favorite illegal drug. What had started as a lark nearly forty years earlier had become the backbone to the county's economy. Throughout the region, and particularly in SoHum, marijuana farming had become a way of life, one that transcended class and generations. "It's what we do here," people would say.

Mare herself had grown a half-dozen plants every year for decades.

But the code of silence surrounding the marijuana industry was such that, until one March evening in 2010, there had never been a public gathering in Southern Humboldt where what people did there was openly discussed.

Sure, for twenty years there was an annual hemp festival, where pot-related books and paraphernalia were sold, and for decades there had been meetings to discuss the actions of law enforcement in the community, but a public discussion about the dependence of the local economy on the black market marijuana crop had never happened before. Up until this moment, it was even considered bad form to ask what someone did for a living in the community. It was just understood.

As she approached the town of Redway, Mare hung a right. She passed the grocery store that most old-timers still called Murrish's, eased the Volvo into a parking spot, and began to shuffle toward the boxy beige building on the hill.

She passed through the front doors of the Mateel Community Center and a giant wooden sculpture of an open hand. Inside, the stage where musicians from around the world came to play shows was empty, but the entire oak floor below was filled with a dozen long banquet tables and an army of folding chairs. On each table were handwritten place cards indicating who should sit there. There were tables for landowners, local government, medical marijuana patients, the press, "Growers," and "Just Curious." There was even a gray metal chair labeled "FBI."

It was a large crowd for Southern Humboldt. Nearly two hundred people were milling about. Instead of picking a table, Mare headed for the fireplace in the back corner that was sculpted to resemble a giant redwood tree trunk and looked as though it should have a cauldron bubbling away inside it. Across the room she spotted her cousin Jewel, who shared her silver hair and warm smile. There were other familiar faces in the crowd—neighbors and friends—and the unfamiliar. Seated at the landowners' table was a woman with long, coppery red hair named Kym Kemp. A third-generation Humboldter, Kemp had been blogging about local marijuana culture since 2007, under the name Redheaded Blackbelt. Her blog posts ranged from photos of local wildflowers and quilts she helped stitch to links to stories about the marijuana industry and flyers of the occasional missing person. Sitting nearby was a man Mare knew named Charley Custer, who was dressed in his trademark Stetson hat and Jesus sandals. Custer had moved to Humboldt from Chicago in 1980 to write a book that he referred to as his "opus dopus." It was, as of yet, incomplete.

Engrossed in a conversation over by the stage was the event's mastermind, Anna "Banana" Hamilton. Hamilton was an outspoken folksinger in her sixties who hosted a monthly talk show on KMUD called *Rant and Rave*. She normally tooled around town in jeans and a baseball cap, but on this evening, she was dressed up, in a lavender velvet top and pearls.

Mare glanced around the room and realized that regardless of where people were sitting, the majority were what she called marijuana moonshiners, just like her.

The irony was that every table was now full except for the growers' table, where only two brave souls had claimed a seat. One of them was Mare's neighbor Syreeta Lux, a sturdy blonde who wore an enormous grin. Lux had lived in the community for decades and figured it was impossible to have a conversation about the future of the marijuana industry if growers were still invisible. It's now or never, she figured, as she pulled her chair up to the empty table. Lux quickly waved over a friend, and wrote "medical" above the word *growers*, to try to get people to feel more at ease. Like Mare, Syreeta Lux recognized many faces of friends, neighbors, and other community members in the crowd who were also growers, but still no one else joined her.

It may have seemed strange that fourteen years after

California passed the nation's first medical marijuana law, which allowed people to grow pot legally with a doctor's recommendation, America's most infamous marijuana growers might be hesitant to claim their heritage, but this was a community that had paid a price for its decades-long rebellion. It had endured annual government raids, and the army itself had once invaded. Then there was the lawless side of the business, the home-invasion rip-offs, and the occasional murder. For decades, to announce oneself as a grower would have been like painting a big target on one's back. The times were indeed changing, but they didn't change quickly in Humboldt.

The event was about to begin, and Syreeta Lux decided to take things a step further. She stood up, held the "Growers" sign high above her head, and commanded the room's attention.

"If anyone is looking for a place to sit, there's lots of room at our table to grow," she announced in a loud, booming voice.

And then she grinned even wider.

From her spot by the fireplace, Mare figured she would let Syreeta represent the female growers. After years of living in the shadows, Mare had no intention of claiming a seat at that table. But when Syreeta stood up and encouraged others to join her, it was as if Mare's feet had a mind of their own, and just like that, she found herself stepping forward. In front of her family, friends, community, elected officials, local and national media, and maybe even the FBI, Mare Abidon shuffled toward the growers' table.

And she wasn't the only one.

"Come on!" Syreeta Lux shouted for others to join them, and they did.

Like some kind of illicit farming coming-out ceremony, more growers stepped into the light. Eventually their numbers swelled to a few dozen, and later they had to retreat to the outdoor patio to have enough space to talk among themselves. But first, from her perch near the stage, Anna Hamilton spoke the words that everyone knew, but no one had yet dared to declare publicly.

"The legalization of marijuana will be the single most devastating economic bust in the long boom-and-bust history of Northern California, impacting local businesses, nonprofit organizations, the workforce, and county tax revenue," she said, pausing for dramatic effect to peer at the crowd over the top of her reading glasses.

As Hamilton and everyone else knew, pot farming was not only a way of life in the region; it was the foundation of the entire economy. People had grown so dependent on the lucrative black market prices that some locals referred to marijuana's illegality as the best government price support program in U.S. history. Prohibition and suppression create risk for growers and artificial scarcity on the market, sending prices and profit margins through the roof.

But that price support system was now at risk.

The U.S. government effectively outlawed marijuana in 1937. Though it is nontoxic and there are no recorded cases in history of anyone ever dying from overdosing on the drug, since the creation of the Controlled Substances Act in 1970 the federal government has classified marijuana as a Schedule I substance. This means the government considers pot more dangerous than cocaine or methamphetamine, with no medical value whatsoever. Many American people are of a different mind. In the late 1990s, starting with California in 1996, states began adopting medical marijuana laws. By the spring of 2010, fourteen states and Washington, D.C., had passed such laws.

These new laws, coupled with a cultural shift toward the acceptance of marijuana on a national level, brought more people into the industry and caused the price of pot on the black market gradually to decline. Marijuana was now a multi-billion-dollar industry in the Golden State, and a measure to legalize and tax it for adult recreational use had just gathered enough signatures to appear on the November ballot.

As Anna Hamilton pointed out that evening, if the measure passed, it could change everything in Humboldt.

"Every member of our society holds a stake in the consequences of legalization," she said, as she began to point to the various tables—to the landowners, educators, members of the business community, and pot growers.

"Did I skip anyone who wants to be recognized tonight?" she asked. "Any representatives from the federal government? I see someone's sitting in that fed chair over there. Is that just a joke?!"

Apparently it was, so Hamilton continued.

If the legalization measure passed, she predicted that the price of marijuana grown outdoors in the sun, the traditional Humboldt way, could drop from its current rate of around $2,000 a pound to as low as $500. If that happened, the effects would be catastrophic. The market would bottom out, affecting growers and everyone who worked for them, which Hamilton estimated to be between fifteen and thirty thousand people in Humboldt County alone.

In a few months' time, the RAND Corporation, a nonprofit think tank, would release a study with a similar prediction. It estimated that the legalization of the production and distribution of marijuana in California could cause prices to drop up to 80 percent.

There was reason to worry in the room, and it wasn't just about economic self-interest. Proceeds from marijuana had not only supported and sustained individuals in the community, but had also helped build local institutions, including a health clinic, the radio station KMUD, and the Mateel Community Center, where the evening's conversation was taking place. Donating earnings from a plant or a pound to these nonprofits, and to the community schools and volunteer fire departments, was how for years many locals paid their "taxes."

All this was poised to change.

"If the value of marijuana drops below a certain level," Hamilton warned, "the state will be faced with the collapse of its rural economies. Businesses will be shuttered, the nonprofit community will be unable to provide services to suddenly displaced peoples, and the golden goose will be dead."

She looked up at the crowd.

"We will all face this economic decline together. For the sake of our region, it is time to begin planning for this upheaval now, together.

"What will we do?" she asked.

There was dead silence.

"We have all the talent and all the answers we need right here in this room."

Among the ideas that bubbled up that evening was an advisory panel of pot growers that would meet with local elected officials to discuss how to regulate their industry. One couple came away from the meeting inspired to form the area's first collective to try to sell organic, artisanal Humboldt pot legally under the state's medical model. Some audience members expressed the long-held fear that legalization would bring the corporatization of the industry and that the market would be flooded with cheap, mass-produced weed, and they wouldn't be able to compete. Others, including a local government official, saw it as an opportunity to take advantage of Humboldt's legendary brand. Across the country and beyond, the Humboldt County name had become deeply linked with pot.

"We've had this name association for thirty or forty years now," County Supervisor Mark Lovelace remarked. "If this is a newly legitimized industry, shouldn't we be looking at capitalizing on that?"

There was talk of creating an appellation, modeled after the world's great wine-growing regions, to designate that local pot was Humboldt homegrown. The way Hamilton saw it, the future of the area was either "appellation or Appalachia." Should marijuana become legal, Humboldt County could become the Napa Valley of Pot, complete with "marijuanaries," where tourists could visit and sample the latest harvest. The business possibilities were endless: "bud and breakfasts," where rooms overlooked fragrant green gardens; a marijuana museum, detailing the history of the area's decades-long experiment in civil disobedience; food and pot pairings at local restaurants; and some kind of four-wheel-drive trolley service, like the limos of the Napa Valley, to cart intoxicated tourists up unpaved roads to tour the pot farms.

"I'm not dying until there's a tasting room in Humboldt County!" a woman with a brown bob and glasses passionately declared.

She was greeted with an enthusiastic round of applause.

That evening, Mare Abidon wasn't worried about the price of pot or how she might brand herself; instead, she was bursting with hope. She had always expected that marijuana would become legal one day, and when it did, she planned to plant big pot bushes in plain sight between the cherry trees around her deck. In fact, she'd never imagined it would take this long. She never really understood the whole War on Drugs, or why the government considered marijuana such a menace. She thought it was great medicine, and even safer than alcohol as a way to unwind at the end of the day.

With the coming legalization, Mare thought that all the jails were going to be emptied of people arrested for pot, and that she and her friends who grew it were finally going to become legitimate members of society.

Much was discussed that night, but what Mare took away, what she'd always remember, was that giddy rush of emotion, the feeling of pure liberation as she stepped into the light and walked toward that growers' table. "It was like crawling out from under a rock that I had been under for decades," she later confessed.

But, of course, not everyone felt that way.

CHAPTER TWO

Crockett

Against the shadowy outline of the mighty redwoods, the speeding Ford pickup looked like a toy powered by some far-off remote control. A balmy, late summer wind whipped through the truck's open window and through the sandy brown hair of the man behind the wheel. It was late, and there was no emergency, but Crockett Randall sped as if his life depended on it. He loved to drive fast. He called it taking an engine to its limit, but it wasn't really about the engine; it was about the adrenaline. The closer Crockett came to death, the more alive he felt, whether it was hurtling down a snow-covered mountain on a snowboard or driving thirty miles over the speed limit on a dark country road.

At thirty-five, Crockett was old enough to know better, but teetering on the edge was part of who he was, and he did it in ways you'd never suspect just by looking at him. Crockett had a strong, square jaw, shy blue eyes, and a permanent tan earned by bobbing around on a surfboard off the

16

North Coast, braving hypothermia and great white sharks in the hope of catching the perfect wave. One of Crockett's greatest gifts was that he possessed the quiet, unassuming presence of someone you could easily forget was in the room.

This chameleon-like quality helped him blend in with the ranchers he worked with at the volunteer fire department back home, and with the men he used to operate heavy equipment with. The aging hippies on the commune where he grew up still accepted him as one of their own, and when the police pulled him over for speeding, which happened at least once a month, usually all Crockett had to do was flash the license that permitted him to drive fire trucks, and the cop would realize he was part of the brotherhood. Then there was the underworld where Crockett made his money, where everything was built on trust and intuition. He belonged to that brotherhood, too.

In many ways, Crockett was the perfect example of the kind of men who migrated to Humboldt County every year. They came from around the country and sometimes from abroad, like miners of old, hoping to strike it rich. In general, these newcomers didn't tend to tithe their earnings with donations to hospice, or spend $1,000 on raffle tickets to support the community school. These newcomers often lived in isolation out in the hills, where they clear-cut hillsides and grew pot. Or they filled buildings with impossibly bright lights and grew their plants indoors, with diesel-powered generators. Crockett was part of this Green Rush, as it was called, but he also came to the marijuana industry honestly.

He was born into it.

The Avenue of the Giants that Crockett raced along was a thirty-mile strip of asphalt named after the redwood forest it meandered through. Back before the state built a four-lane highway through most of Humboldt County, the Avenue was the main thoroughfare north. Now it was a rambling country road, a parallel scenic route that offered tourists a way to submerge themselves in the splendor of the big trees without having to leave their cars.

Sometimes when Crockett roared down the Avenue with his coworker Zavie, with "My Dick," by Mickey Avalon, blasting on the stereo, Crockett would wonder about the tourists they passed, with their RVs and cameras. Did they have any idea what was going on here? But then he and Zavie would arrive at the South Fork of the Eel River and park so that Crockett could catapult off the truck's tailgate into the water—the "Humboldt diving board," he called it—and the sweat of the morning's labor and that very thought itself would be washed away with the current.

At this late hour, Crockett's destination wasn't the Eel, which was running low and dry beyond the trees. He was headed back to the cabin on the hill, to the place where he'd been on lockdown for the past few weeks. An hour or so earlier, he had snuck off to eat at the Avenue Café in Miranda. He dined at his usual spot, at the redwood slab counter. Under dim lights, he ate chicken parmigiana and scrolled through friends' Facebook updates on his laptop. A lone highway patrol officer sat a few seats away. After the officer left, Crockett peered out the window to make sure the cop was headed in the opposite direction, then settled up his bill and tipped the waitress. Crockett had to get back to the cabin. Every moment he was away there was a risk that someone could come and take everything he had spent the past five months working toward.

Crockett turned off the Avenue and gunned up a hill. He left the redwoods behind as he climbed higher into a dense forest of Douglas fir and tan oak. After a few miles of twists and turns, he arrived at a driveway that was sealed with a metal gate. The sign that hung from it read "No Trespassing." Crockett's fingers moved nimbly across the padlock. He lifted up the heavy chain, and the gate swung open.

Dust billowed up around the truck as Crockett bounced down the bumpy dirt road, the kind that wore cars out before their time and felt so far from civilization it seemed like it might lead straight into the African bush. There were two more padlocked gates and two more warning signs: "Private." "Keep Out." Unpaved roads reminded Crockett of the commune he grew up on. But those roads had been tamer; grizzled men never hauled giant trees down them, and they didn't have Humboldt's foreboding barriers or signs.

The cabin was located down a steep grade past the final gate. As Crockett pulled up in front of it, the headlights on his truck illuminated the small square building and the tree line just beyond. He killed the engine, and everything went black. After a few seconds his eyes adjusted, and it was as though the dark sky had been pierced with a million holes. The stars guided him behind the cabin, where he flipped on the generator, a necessity for life off the electrical grid.

Its diesel-powered rumble broke the stillness of the country night.

Obscured by the darkness beyond the cabin was a greenhouse full of mature marijuana plants. Deeper in the wood were even more greenhouses full of hundreds of plants. When all was said and done, the pot grown in them was expected to fetch close to $1 million.

Inside the cabin, Crockett kicked off his flip-flops, settled into the couch, and prepared to roll a joint. He operated in a near-permanent state of stoned, which didn't make him lethargic or giggly, like those idiots in the movies; it just made him quieter than usual. Whenever Crockett tried to stop smoking, he found himself unable to sleep. The bed where he spent his nights was directly across the room. To his right, the kitchen area was piled high with dirty dishes. Past the kitchen, a door led to a tiny bathroom, where the toilet was filled by a hose that ran through the window. The shower was outside.

The cabin was rustic, but it was downright palatial compared with how some people lived during the growing season. It could get pretty rugged in the Humboldt Hills. Some people stayed in buildings so shoddy that light seeped through the boards. Others lived in tents and trailers. Many places didn't have indoor plumbing or a toilet and a hose, which meant people had to head to the outhouse or into the woods to do their business.

Crockett knew he was fortunate, and he was comfortable enough being by himself, but sometimes he missed seeing familiar faces every day, and having a smooth, curvy body to press up against at night. When he moved to Humboldt that spring, he figured it would be good to take a break from women for a while, but now he wished he had brought one along. Zavie also missed female companionship. Sometimes the two schemed about opening up a brothel together. They figured if they could provide their fellow growers with hookers and blow, they'd be able to take all their money. Zavie had gotten so lonely lately that he'd started lusting after the seventeen-year-old who cleaned their weed.

The trimmer girl, as they called her, had manicured the pot Crockett was about to smoke. With her Fiskars sewing scissors, she had shaped the bud into the tight, compact, grape-size nugget he stuck in his herb grinder. The metal prongs minced the flower and infused the cabin with the smell of sweet pine. He then poured the contents into the fold of a rolling paper and began rubbing it back and forth between his thumbs and index fingers to form a joint.

Crockett's favorite kind of weed at the moment was Blue Dream, but the joint he was rolling was filled with O.G. Kush. Marijuana comes in different varieties, called strains. Most strains are crosses between the two primary species *Cannabis sativa* and *Cannabis indica*. Marijuana growers create hybrids of the two and give them names that have never passed through a marketing department: Headband. Sour Diesel. Green Crack. Earlier in the summer, a strain with the unforgettable name of God's Pussy won the *High Times* Medical Cannabis Cup in San Francisco. (Due to public backlash, it was renamed Vortex a few days later.) The O.G. Kush that Crockett was about to smoke was a particularly popular strain. Rappers composed odes to it, and there was strong demand for it on the black market. This particular bud had come from a recent harvest Crockett and Zavie grew inside a house their boss Frankie owned near Garberville.

While there is no one way to grow pot, as growers are fond of saying, there are basically two: inside, under high-wattage lights, or outdoors in the sun. Marijuana grown indoors can be harvested every two to three months. Outdoor plants are traditionally harvested once a year, in the fall. New methods involving light deprivation, or "depping," trick the plant into flowering earlier and can lead to multiple outdoor harvests. Frankie required that Crockett and Zavie grow a small indoor garden to ensure a steady flow of cash. The windfall, however, would come from the outdoor garden on the hill, the one Crockett spent his days and nights guarding from authorities, and thieves, the garden that was located in greenhouses in a clearing in the forest near the cabin where he was now sitting.

———

Like the children of Humboldt's growers, marijuana had always been part of Crockett's life. His first memory was of being on a plane with his mother. They were leaving Arizona, where Crockett's father was sitting in jail, busted for smuggling pot across the Mexican border. Decades later, Crockett would have no memory of the man. He didn't even carry his last name.

In the late 1970s, Crockett's mother brought him to live

on a commune north of San Francisco. Like Humboldt, his corner of Marin County was a place that had been settled by Old World ranchers and fishermen, and then, in the 1960s and '70s, by the New World counterculture. On the commune, Crockett was first introduced to the tall, fragrant plant that would play such a big role in his life. As a young boy, he loved pressing the smooth peppercorn-size seeds into soil and adding water. Little green shoots seemed to pop out of the wet earth almost instantly, like magic beanstalks.

When he started elementary school, his mother supported them by selling pot and cocaine to local fishermen. Crockett knew by then that it was a secret he must keep. He worried about coming to school smelling of the plant during harvest time, or that someone might notice how the plastic bags that carried his sandwiches had tiny green flakes in the corners, remnants of what they once held. By the time he was seventeen, Crockett was selling pot in a local trailer park. Though he has held other jobs over the years, he has been involved in the marijuana industry in some way ever since.

Crockett had known Frankie since elementary school. They rode the bus together when they were little, and in high school they carpooled and smoked pot before class. Later, they were briefly roommates. Then Frankie fell in love with a girl from Southern Humboldt and moved there to join her. He found work in the marijuana industry, as men who are brought into the community often do. He started out working for others, and moved up fast. Frankie lived in the Bay Area now, with a new girlfriend, but owned property in Humboldt, and a shiny new Mercedes. Most important, Frankie had reached the stage where he could afford to pay people to work for him.

Frankie's timing had been fortuitous. After fifteen years of operating heavy equipment, Crockett was ready for a change. When Frankie approached him with the job offer, Crockett agreed to move to Humboldt to manage the season's marijuana crop for a cut of the earnings, somewhere around $100,000 in cash. Like sharecropping in the South, the arrangement is called *partnering* in marijuana culture, and is common among growers who live somewhere else or just prefer to pay someone else to dig holes, stake up plants, water, fertilize, set mouse and rat traps, walk waterlines, and handle all the other manual labor that goes along with pot farming.

Crockett had never lived in Humboldt before, nor had he ever grown a giant outdoor garden, but it sounded like a good chunk of money, and he did have experience growing a few plants in a spare bedroom back home. He had also spent years working as a middleman, or broker, as they call it in the business, connecting friends with buyers and taking a cut off the top. Growing for Frankie sounded like a lucrative deal, until Crockett learned about the Zavie element.

Zavie was a tall, skinny guy, with slightly buck teeth and pencil-thin dreadlocks. He was born in Jamaica, the lovechild of a hippie mother and a Rastafarian father. He and Frankie met in junior college, where they used to party and snort cocaine together. Zavie was a functioning drunk, and would party for days on booze and coke until he passed out. Recently, Zavie had gotten a DUI and was facing a few months of jail time. Zavie's arrival on the scene meant that Crockett wouldn't have to work so hard, and at first he was happy to have someone to share the load with, until he came to understand just who that someone was.

The garden that Crockett and Zavie were growing for Frankie up near the cabin was big. While it was legal under California law to grow a small number of plants for medical use, gardens over 100 plants risked stiff mandatory sentences under federal law. Theirs was many times that, and its flowers were destined not for medical patients at dispensaries, but for the black market that for decades had ensured that marijuana farmers were among the world's richest. At various times throughout the 1980s pot was worth more per ounce than gold. In the early 1990s, some master growers in Humboldt earned as much as $6,000 a pound for their outdoor crop.

Government price support program, indeed.

Then, in 1996, Proposition 215, the Compassionate Use Act, became law, and medical marijuana patients were allowed to grow their own. Since the law was written so loosely that just about anyone could become a medical marijuana patient, more people entered the growing game, especially in recent years, as the economy tanked. Pot wasn't just an Emerald Triangle product anymore. People around the state began growing more of it in their garages, attics, and backyards, and prices on the black market began to spiral downward. Now, in 2010, a statewide initiative called

Proposition 19, the Regulate, Control, and Tax Cannabis Act, would, if passed by voters in November, legalize pot outright. It was the reason for the community meeting Mare had attended. Crockett's boss and his friends were also worried. Frankie was completely against legalization. His motto was "I'm not in this for the money, I'm in this for a lot of money." A sticker on the wall at his house summed up his feelings and the feelings of many other growers: "Save Humboldt County, Keep Pot Illegal."

The vote was just over two months away, and Crockett still hadn't made up his mind yet about legalization. On one hand, he liked the idea of drastic changes in history, and ending marijuana prohibition sounded cool. On the other, he listened faithfully to the radio news program *Democracy Now!*, he was partial to conspiracy theories, and his distrust of government ran deep. Sometimes Crockett would tell people he played both sides of the War on Drugs. He knew that growers supported the economy with all the money they laundered, but there was also another side that he didn't agree with, the whole prison industrial complex, with its judges, and prison guards and police who earned money by locking people away. The government had spent $41 billion that year alone fighting the War on Drugs, according to a study by the libertarian Cato Institute. It was a war Crockett knew could never be won.

He also wondered how he and his friends would make a living in a world where pot was legal and no longer as lucrative. With legalization, would companies such as Philip Morris plant acres of ganja in the Central Valley? Or, worse yet, what if China started growing pot for export? They'd be selling it at dollar stores. These thoughts had all occurred to Crockett, but he put them out of his mind as he lay on the couch and finished his joint to the tinny sound of the "Hotel California" remix playing on his laptop.

First, he had to guard the crop and get through harvest. Then he had to get paid. And then maybe he could start thinking about legalization and his future. He already had a five-year plan. By the time he was forty, he wanted to get his pilot's license, find his father, and build a little cabin on the commune where he grew up.

On this late August night, the marijuana flowers outside were beginning to fill out and were near their resiny peaks. It was a time when sheriff's deputies might come to your gate to make sure your medical paperwork was in order. And it was rip-off season, when thieves could make off with a year's crop in one fell swoop. Paranoia permeated the hills of Humboldt this time of year. It explained the pit bulls in the back of the trucks around town and the brisk sales of motion-detecting cameras and alarm systems at the Security Store up in the Meadows Business Park (the "insecurity" store, as some people called it). The irony was that while most outsiders feared stumbling upon armed growers in Humboldt, most growers feared being stumbled upon by armed men themselves. It wasn't only money they risked losing. Media reports about violence in the community were often exaggerated, but the sad truth of the matter was that people had been losing their lives over marijuana in Humboldt County for almost as long as it had been grown there.

The first known bust of a pot grower in Humboldt County went down on September 29, 1960, north of the city of Arcata, near a stream of water known as Strawberry Creek. After a multiple-hour stakeout that morning, a sheriff's deputy arrested and charged a man named Eugene Crawford with growing a little more than two dozen, three-inch-high pot plants. Crawford had arrived at the scene with a box and shovel in hand; he said he was going to dig worms. He was found guilty after a three-day trial the following year. A decade later, the first recorded marijuana-related killing occurred.

October 4, 1970, was a Sunday, and outside the dairy town of Ferndale, Patrick Berti came to check out two four-foot-tall marijuana plants that were basking in the fall sun. Berti was twenty-two, had grown up in Ferndale, and had just been accepted into law school in San Diego. He examined the plants, unaware that he was being watched. For, hidden in the bushes nearby, was an ambitious young sheriff's deputy on a stakeout. Larry Lema was also from Ferndale and had known Berti for years. At one point, Berti held up a marijuana branch that the deputy would later say he mistook for a weapon. Lema drew his gun and fired, ripping a hole in Berti's chest.

As he lay bleeding on the riverbank, Berti recognized the man who'd pulled the trigger.

"Christ, Larry," he cried. "You've shot me."

Then Patrick Berti died. The pot plants didn't even belong to him, but to a friend. Berti had come to the river that day to marvel at their height. A Humboldt County grand jury later ruled Berti's shooting "justifiable homicide."

In the decades that followed, there were more pot-related deaths, and some stood out more than others, like that of Kathy Davis, the social worker with the heart of gold whose 1982 murder during a robbery at her home shattered the innocence of the community. Then there was the nineteen-year-old boy, and member of the second generation, who was shot to death at a local swimming hole during a deal gone wrong. There were also people who disappeared, leaving their family and friends in a perpetual state of unknowing. The community became wary and distrusting of outsiders, of anyone they didn't know. But business continued, and in some ways it was amazing that there weren't more murders, given the hundreds of millions of dollars in cash exchanged every year in deals that were often nothing more than "a handshake on a dusty road," as the local song goes.

But then again, almost everyone seemed to know of someone who had been killed.

Though Humboldt County has a low violent-crime rate compared to the rest of the state, in 2012 the Humboldt County Sheriff's Office analyzed the past eight years of data on local homicides, and this is what they found: Of the thirty-eight murders committed during that period, twenty-three, or 70 percent, were drug-related. The drug was usually marijuana. The sheriff noticed that these homicides were not tales of "reefer madness"; assassins hopped up on pot were not driving around looking for innocent prey. Most of the murders were business violence—say, a skirmish over wages or somebody getting shot during a rip-off. During that same period in Napa County, which has a similar population size and whose economy is based on a legal intoxicant—alcohol—there were only eight murders, and just one was marijuana-related.

When you worked outside the law, it seemed the disputes were settled there, too.

Crockett knew since childhood that the potential for violence and rip-offs were part of the business, and Frankie had told him before he moved up to the cabin, "If the rippers come, don't risk your life. Get off the hill."

But Crockett had other plans.

Hidden under the tangle of blankets on his unmade bed was a loaded .22-caliber handgun. It was silver with a black handle, and weighed heavy in his hand. Crockett had too much riding on this. He had quit his job and worked too hard in that garden just to let it all disappear. If the rippers came, Crockett planned to stand his ground. It wasn't about the plants. It never was. It was about the money.

After Crockett exhaled a final cloud of smoke, he headed back outside. The main garden was located farther out on the property. Dust billowed up behind him as he sped along in a Yamaha Rhino, an off-road vehicle that looks like a mini dune buggy. It was close to midnight, and there was only darkness and trees and the high-pitched hum of the Rhino's engine.

When he pulled up at the final gate, Crockett killed the motor on the Rhino, and the lights went out. Again, it was pitch black until the four enormous greenhouses came into view. They were covered in translucent white polyurethane, which gave them a ghostly glow. The three on the right were cylindrical-shaped and about a hundred feet long. From above they must have looked like enormous joints. The fourth was square and about twice the size of the cabin. The whole setup looked like a commercial nursery, which, in a way, it was—an illegal commercial nursery.

Crockett unlocked the gate and strode toward the nearest greenhouse. The thick, musky scent of marijuana hung heavy in the air. The plant's trademark odor was often compared to a skunk's spray; it was the smell that had led to a million busts. He swung open the door of the cabin-shaped greenhouse to have a look at the girls, as growers call female marijuana plants. They were still there, lined up obediently in tidy rows.

They were the same strain he had smoked earlier, O.G. Kush. But whereas the plants he and Zavie grew under bright lights in the house would reach only a few feet tall before they flowered, sun and time coaxed these ladies to heights of around ten feet. Though it was dark, their shadowy shape revealed an industrial uniformity. While many outdoor plants are large and unruly, these were tall and skinny and manicured in a fiercely attentive way, like *premier cru* grapevines.

A few days earlier, Crockett and Zavie had gone through and removed the larger leaves on the plants and tied the heaviest branches to wooden stakes with blue plastic ribbon. While marijuana was known throughout the world for its serrated five-finger leaf, it is the dense, odorous flowers that produce the mind-altering high. As the flower clusters, known as "buds," thickened nearing harvest, the plastic tape and stakes would prevent branches from snapping under their growing weight. O.G. Kush was known among smokers and brokers for its distinct smell and high. Among growers, it was also known for having a weak stem and being prone to mold. The blue tape would help support the stems. As for the mold, there was nothing Crockett could do about that but pray.

He chuckled as he surveyed the blue tape that snaked through the plant in front of him. How it was tied said so much about his and Zavie's differences. Crockett's tape was pulled tight and ran in mathematically straight lines, while Zavie's zigzagged haphazardly around the plants' branches like an unraveled ball of yarn.

Crockett shut the greenhouse door and did a quick walk around the other structures. Between each one was a row of heirloom tomatoes, bell peppers, chard, and beets. It was silly, but Frankie had insisted that Crockett and Zavie grow the vegetables. In case someone buzzed the greenhouses with a plane, Frankie somehow thought they'd think it was a veggie farm. The veggie garden took a lot of work to put in, and while they were doing it, Crockett grumbled to Frankie, "Fuck man, we want to be dope growers, not vegetable growers."

In all, there were around seven hundred marijuana plants

inside the various greenhouses that dotted the property. Because they were hidden behind a thin layer of polyurethane and weren't exposed to the full sun, the plants wouldn't reach the epic proportions some growers were famous for. As with all gardening or farming, the potency and yield of a pot plant came down to the green of a grower's thumb. Multiple-pound plants weren't uncommon among seasoned growers, and one old-timer was rumored to have grown a single monster plant that produced thirteen pounds of pot one year, thanks to his special fertilizer.

Come harvest, Crockett hoped his plants would each produce at least half a pound of pot. One of his connections had promised to pay $3,400 a pound, which meant that after it had been cut, dried, and processed, the pot grown in these greenhouses would net close to $1 million in cash. But that was still a couple of months away. So much could happen before then. Rippers could come. The cops could pay a visit. If the legalization measure passed, and the RAND prediction was true, the market could crash. In the meantime, Crockett would sit in the cabin and guard the crop with his life.

It was late, and he had to be back to water the garden early the next morning. Crockett started up the Rhino, revved its tiny engine, and sped off into the darkness in a cloud of fast-moving dirt.

It was only a matter of days before someone would be shot in a remote Humboldt garden filled with emerald green plants much like his.

CHAPTER THREE

Emma

Emma Worldpeace had just finished up a day's work as a sales associate at Chico Sports LTD when she noticed the missed calls. They were from her little sister, Lisa. It was odd that Lisa had called a few times. Though the sisters were close, they weren't in touch often. Emma decided to call her back as soon as she got home. She hopped on her bike and began the short ride back to the house she shared with her boyfriend, Ethan.

It was early on the evening of August 26, 2010. The dense, dry heat that could make the Central Valley city of Chico feel like a brick oven was just beginning to subside as Emma pedaled down Arbutus Avenue toward the sage-green suburban home she shared with Ethan and a room-mate. Emma was twenty-three years old, with pale skin and a smattering of freckles. She had her father's button nose and wide, doe-like brown eyes, though the first thing everyone noticed about her was her hair, which hung in shoulder-length ringlets and was the russet color redwood needles turn after they fall from the tree. Emma's legs pumped up and down like pistons. She was an avid cyclist and regularly rode at least fifteen hours a week.

After stashing her bike in a shed behind the house, where there were enough bikes to start a small rental business, Emma stopped to kiss her boyfriend. Ethan, a tall, athletic thirty-four-year-old, was drinking a beer with a buddy under the shade tree in the backyard.

Only then did Emma think to pick up her phone and return her sister's call. Lisa was two years younger. Of her five siblings, Lisa was the only one with whom she shared both parents, though Emma considered all her siblings equal. Lisa also used to be the only one who shared Emma's hippie last name, though she had dumped it a few years earlier for the flashier-sounding name of an Italian sports car.

"Hey, girl!" Emma said when her sister picked up.

Lisa sounded strange.

"Did you hear about Mike?" she asked.

"No."

"I don't know exactly what's going on, or if it's true or not," Lisa said hurriedly, the words tumbling out of her mouth. "But basically it sounds like there were some guys living on his property and there was some kind of a fight, and they say he shot someone and has been taken into custody."

After trying to reassure her sister that everything would be okay, Emma hung up the phone, cracked open her laptop, and began scanning the local papers back in Humboldt.

There was a lot of news online about the shooting, and it wasn't good.

"At least one man was severely injured in a shootout in Kneeland last night, apparently in a marijuana-related dispute," *The North Coast Journal* reported.

They were calling it the Kneeland Shooting, and the details were grisly. A forty-year-old Guatemalan immigrant named Mario Roberto Juarez Madrid had been shot and killed in an enormous marijuana garden in a place called Kneeland, in the hills outside Eureka. Another man had been shot in the face and back and had stumbled onto a California Department of Forestry base early that morning.

The prime suspect was Mikal Xylon Wilde, age twenty-eight. He'd been arrested later that morning while driving his big green truck on a road near where the shooting took place. In the mug shot that had been released, Mikal's head was shaved, his beefy shoulders bulged out of a tank top, and he stared blankly at the camera. It was a face that was deeply familiar to Emma. She'd known Mike since childhood. They had been friends; then her mother and his father had children together, and he became family.

Emma considered him her brother.

She scanned the stories for clues to what had happened, searching for anything that might lead her to believe that Mike didn't do it. According to the news reports, Mike had hired three men to tend to a marijuana garden of more than 1,500 plants. The two survivors told police that Mike had recently changed their work agreement and told them he could no longer afford to bring them food, or gas for the irrigation truck, and that they'd have to water the plants by hand. The men had balked at the new conditions, and found their way to a phone, where they called someone to come pick them up. When Mike found out, they said he returned with a gun and opened fire.

A man was dead, another injured, and Mike was in jail. Fear, sadness, anger—so many emotions bubbled up inside Emma. She felt a lump in her throat, and her eyes started to burn, but she fought back the tears, and the urge to go running to Ethan. After all, one of her coping mechanisms during times of crisis was not to talk. She had learned long ago to keep her stories to herself.

It wasn't until after Ethan's friend left that Emma pulled her boyfriend aside and told him the news.

"There was an incident involving my brother Mike," she said. "I don't know if it's true or not, but according to the reports, there was some kind of fight that had to do with plants or supplies, and one guy was shot and killed."

"Oh my god, I'm so sorry," Ethan said, as he enveloped her in a giant hug.

Like seeds sown in a garden long ago, the roots of this story about growing up in marijuana culture began years back, during a winter rainstorm in the hills of Southern Humboldt.

———

It was February 1987.

"The baby is coming!" she hollered.

She had long dark hair and a childlike face. Her name was Linda Rivas, but she'd called herself Sage ever since she met a shaman in Harvard Square years earlier who told her she should change her name, go west, and join the Rainbow Tribe. Sage had already given birth twice, and knew it was time, even before the pressure began to come in those rhythmic waves known as contractions.

"Hey guys! It's coming now!"

The baby's father came running. His name was Stephen Frech. He and Sage had met a few years earlier while she was living in the Resting Oak Village, a settlement of old vacation cabins on the Eel River. Frech was a short, stout man with an enormous curly red beard. He looked as though he hailed from the Hobbits' Shire. In reality, he was a Volkswagen mechanic from rural New Jersey who was known around Southern Humboldt as EZ Out, after his special method for popping windshields out of cars. His technique involved sitting in the driver's seat and pushing against the glass with his stubby legs until the window popped out with a satisfying crack.

EZ Out set Sage up in the bed next to the woodstove in the living room and rubbed her back, while word was sent out to contact the midwife. Since there was no phone line in the house, someone had to drive to the top of the dirt road, a few miles away, to get enough of a connection on the CB radio to let the midwife know the baby was on its way.

As the hours passed, the rain fell steadily and the contractions came harder and faster. A small crowd gathered in the living room to witness the baby's arrival, but still there was no midwife.

When it became obvious the baby was coming, midwife or not, a small power struggle ensued between EZ Out and the unborn baby's godmother, Tie-Dye Debrah, over who was going to catch the newborn as it entered the world. When the moment finally came, in front of a warm fire, surrounded by loved ones, a baby girl was born. Her father and godmother still hadn't settled who would hold her first and started pulling on her.

"Wait a minute!" her mother wailed. "Stop! The cord is still attached!"

When the umbilical cord was cut, the newborn was wrapped in a tie-dye rainbow blanket. She was bald and breathtakingly innocent. Her parents named her Emma Rosa.

As for her last name, around the time of her birth, Sage and EZ Out couldn't agree on whose name to use. One day in town, Sage got to talking to a man named Barefoot George, who used to live in a school bus and led a decidedly shoeless existence. Sage explained her predicament to him.

"I don't know what I'm going to do," she told him.

"Why don't you call her Worldpeace?" Barefoot George suggested. "There's no reason to fight over a name. Give her the name Worldpeace, and there will be peace over this."

Sage liked the sound of that, and the idea that every time people heard her daughter's last name, they would have to think about peace on earth, even if just for a moment.

So Emma Worldpeace was bestowed her unusual last

name, one that she would carry into adulthood and that in many ways would help define her. As she would one day explain, "It's hard to be an asshole when your last name is Worldpeace."

———

When Emma was still a baby, the family moved to a new home. The house was a two-story geodesic dome on eighty acres located deep in the rolling, grassy hills of a community called Salmon Creek. The building was covered in shingles and looked like a giant orb. The main living space was a round, open room with a kitchen that looped around to the left. It had giant windows that were framed by the grapevines that grew outside, and rugs were spread across the floor for people to sprawl upon.

Downstairs, there was a secret passageway. The entrance was next to the bedroom where Lisa, Emma's younger sister, was born. In the cool, dark root cellar where Sage stored her preserved pickles and jellies, a hidden panel opened and led to a crawl space that wound up through the walls. It was a favorite spot for Emma and her siblings when they played hide-and-seek.

Life at the dome, as they called it, was a world unto itself. The highway was a forty-five-minute drive away, and "town," Garberville or Redway, an hour away. Not that they ever needed to go anywhere. The property was a wonderland where just walking to the top of the two-mile-long driveway was an all-day adventure. Snacks grew on the pear, fig, and walnut trees that dotted the property, and what seemed like the world's biggest mulberry tree towered behind the goat shed. Up a steep hill from the dome, in a giant oak, someone had built a tree house that could make a child's heart sing; it had a working woodstove, a small deck, and a stained-glass window.

Like most everyone in their community, Sage and EZ Out supported themselves by growing pot. For Emma, this was as normal as if her parents raised cows or worked in an office. Sometimes she'd join her mom and siblings and carry water deep into the woods to water the plants, which were hidden under the forest canopy. It didn't occur to her then that there were risks to the work, or that her parents could go to jail for what they were doing.

That realization would come later, in a shockingly sudden way.

At the time, there was a more visible shadow to life at the dome. EZ Out was a drinker. He could go through twenty-four beers in a day. Sage had come to realize that she couldn't count on him to help with the children or the crop. She kicked him out, and EZ Out began the deeper descent into alcoholism that would land him in San Quentin State Prison for drunk driving a few months later.

Around this same time, Sage figured it was time to buy a property of her own. She found a house in another small hill community, called Ettersburg. Morning Glory Manor, as the house was called, was located down a dirt road lined with twisted red manzanita. The driveway meandered past the barn where Emma's older siblings, Aia and Omar, slept, and then the horse corral and vegetable garden, before it turned up an impossibly steep grade. At the crest of the hill, next to the shed where the generator was stored, Morning Glory Manor stood on stilts. It was three flights of stairs to the front door, which was framed on each side by stained-glass windows depicting the house's namesake periwinkle flower.

Morning Glory Manor was located off the electrical grid, which meant the generator that provided the family's electricity had to be filled with propane from time to time. Firewood needed to be chopped and stacked, and the pump that brought water from the creek to the house had to be turned on and off at least once a week.

And so Emma Worldpeace continued her life completely off the map.

Shortly after moving to the new house, Sage began dating an accountant and jazz guitarist named Jim Wilde. Jim was a quiet, older man with a son named Mikal, who was the same age as Emma's twelve-year-old sister, Aia. Emma looked up to Mike in that admiring way younger kids do. He was allowed to eat sugary cereal, and he had a TV in his room, and a stereo on which he'd blast Snoop Dogg and Too $hort. Mike became her stepbrother, and in many ways, he treated Emma as a big brother should. He gave her rides on his four-wheeler, and let her hang out with him and his friends. If he thought she was being too nerdy or too straight, he would affectionately refer to her as "Lisa Simpson," as in "Don't be such a Lisa Simpson." He also introduced her to alcohol. The first time Emma ever drank was with Mike. They stole some of Jim's beers from the fridge, smuggled them out of the house, and sipped them in the woods.

Mike was all about adventure. One summer morning, when Sage brought Emma and Lisa over for a visit, he suggested the girls join him on a hike. They set out with Mike's sheepdog, Rudy, on an old logging road. They followed the road until they arrived at an open meadow that had a giant fir tree standing in the middle. The meadow looked out on tiny Salmon Creek School. The velvet green Bear Buttes Mountain towered in the distance. Pushing on, they came upon a patch of hillside that had been scorched by fire. In the middle of it stood a trailer that had been licked black by the flames. Whoever had lived in the trailer seemed to have left in a hurry. Inside the charred cabinets were dishes and dish soap, and there were clothes left in the bedroom. The trailer fascinated the three explorers, as did the singed pot plants they found in a ditch outside, dry and crispy, but unmistakable.

Emma, Mike, and Lisa were so engrossed in their discovery that they didn't notice the fog rolling in off the Pacific and over the ridgetop behind them. Cool and thick, it blanketed everything in its mist. By the time the group decided to head for home, they didn't get very far before they realized they were lost. With the fog swirling around them, they couldn't figure out which direction they needed to head. They searched for landmarks, like the school, which was located just below the Wilde house, but the mist was so dense they could barely see a few feet ahead of them.

Lisa started to panic.

"It's going to get dark, we are going to get eaten by coyotes, and we are going to die!" she wailed.

Mike tried to reassure her that everything was going to be okay and that they just needed to make a plan.

In the meantime, Rudy, the sheepdog, had wandered off.

"Ruuuuudy," they called her name, but their voices seemed quickly lost in the mist that swirled around them.

When Rudy finally appeared, she was panting and exhausted. Everyone was exhausted. They had been out for hours. They hadn't brought snacks, water, or a flashlight, and the sun was setting. In hindsight, it was a terribly planned expedition.

Then Mike had the idea to send Rudy home. Maybe the dog had an internal homing device.

"Go get it, go home, Rudy!" they ordered.

At first, the dog ignored them while she caught her breath, but then she lifted herself onto her stubby little legs and headed over the hill through the fog. Sure enough, Rudy led them home. Like a good, confident older brother, Mike had known what to do, and Emma would look to him for answers.

In Ettersburg, Sage continued to support her family by growing marijuana. The plants were grown in a greenhouse near the barn where Aia and Omar lived. By then, everyone referred to them as the tomato plants, as in "We have to move the tomato plants" or "It's time to water the tomato plants." Emma knew by then not to talk about them to other people. They had become a secret.

Sometimes, in the evenings, Sage would pile her children

in her red Nissan Pathfinder and drive down the Briceland–Shelter Cove Road toward town. She often took Emma and her newborn son, John. In January of 1995, Sage had given birth to her fifth child in conditions very similar to Emma's arrival: at home, during a storm, with no midwife.

On those evening drives, the destination was almost always the same. Sage would park at the bottom of a dirt road near a grove of redwood trees, and with her children in the backseat, she would deal pot.

Most of the time, this meant a lot of waiting. Emma would sit in the back next to her baby brother and read a book. Sometimes she'd listen to music with her mom. She never felt scared or stressed. Eventually the buyer would show up, usually nice, clean-cut older men from the city. They'd sit in the front seat with Sage and exchange a few words. Sage would pull out a plastic bag and show them what she had for sale. They'd smell it, and maybe they'd roll a joint and smoke a little to test the wares. Then they'd discuss the price with Sage.

Often, the buyer would look in the backseat and say a friendly hello to Emma.

"How are you?" they'd ask, and maybe they'd coo at baby John.

Then, in the shadow of the giant trees, Sage and her customers would settle on a price, and marijuana and money would change hands.

Later, people would begin to wonder about the price their children paid for growing up under a cloak of secrecy, and how damaging it was not being able to say what their parents did for a living, carrying the weight of a secret that could send family members to jail. Some would ask themselves how could they expect their children to obey the laws of society if they didn't obey them themselves.

Just as every generation rebels against the one that came before, the children of hippies with loose boundaries and a cash economy would find their own unexpected way to reject the values of their parents.

But on those dark nights, with a fresh wad of cash for groceries and mortgage payments, such thoughts were far from Sage's mind. With a backseat full of sleepy children, she would start up the Pathfinder and head for home.

It was all too easy to forget when all your friends and neighbors did it, too, that this seemingly peaceful farming lifestyle was illegal, and that when one got caught and the law came down, it would be with crushing force.

CHAPTER FOUR

Bob

The sixteen men filed past in a straight line. Their size and coloring varied, but the orange jumpsuits of the California Department of Corrections and Rehabilitation rendered them all identical: low-level inmates from the Eel River Conservation Camp. Since 1967, the Corrections Department and the Department of Forestry had operated the "con camp" near the Redway garbage dump. It was a place where prisoners could serve out their sentences picking up trash along the highway, thinning out the forest, or cutting lines in the ground to contain wildfires during fire season.

On this fall day in 2010, one of the prisoners lugged a chainsaw; another balanced a weed whacker on his shoulder. There was brush to destroy on a bluff that overlooked Garberville, Highway 101, and the Eel River Valley. In places, the coyote brush and Scotch broom had grown so high it reached the men's chests. But the problem wasn't really the brush; it was the people who had been living in it.

Deputy Bob Hamilton of the Humboldt County Sheriff's Department stood on the bluff next to Sergeant Kenny Swithenbank, and watched the men file past. Some made eye contact, but most just stared straight ahead.

"Thanks, guys!" Bob called out cheerfully.

The acre of overgrown brush that surrounded the men made for a secluded spot for the homeless to camp over the summer. It was clear now of people and debris, save for a pair of black boots, a butter knife jammed into an oak tree, and an oil drum full of concrete. The idea was that cutting back the brush now would make it easier to avoid a repeat next summer.

Bob had been with the department for four years, Kenny for more than twenty, and neither had ever seen it this bad. No one could pinpoint when exactly the first homeless drifters, vagabonds, or transients, as the deputies called them, started drifting into town. Some old-timers attributed their arrival to a story that ran in the marijuana magazine *High Times* back in the 1980s that mentioned the need for seasonal labor in the area. One thing was for sure, this year the transients had flocked to Garberville and Redway in record numbers.

It was like the end of the gold rush.

With the legalization vote looming, maybe transients figured it was their last chance to experience the marijuana heartland before everything changed, like visiting Cuba before the death of Fidel. Whatever the reason for the influx, the transients were many, and they shared a worn, dusty look as they panhandled up and down Main Street, walked their dogs on rope leashes, and swilled booze from paper bags at the Veterans Park in Garberville, which one local had taken to calling "Crusty Park" in their honor.

The majority of the calls the Sheriff's Department received over the summer were complaints about these people. Back at the station, they kept a file marked "Suspects Warned." It contained photos of ripped-up sleeping bags, trash, human excrement, and mug shots of grizzled, broken-looking souls, including one man who looked eerily like Charles Manson. Whenever Bob asked a transient why he or she had come to Garberville, the answer was almost always the same: to get a job in the marijuana industry. The irony wasn't lost on Bob. He knew most growers didn't hire outsiders, especially marginal ones off the street.

"There's nothing here for them," he would say with a shake of his head as he passed a man with a tattered knapsack on Main Street. "They come here looking for trimming jobs that no one is ever going to give them."

As he approached fifty, Bob's light brown hair was starting to thin on top, but his vision was still hawklike, and he could spot a marijuana garden a mile away or a child without a seat belt in a passing car. Tall and broad, Bob carried himself in the bumbling manner of someone who reached his height at an early age, and he had a goofy personality to match. He was the kind of guy who talked to cats, mooed at cows, and might crack a joke while he was arresting you. At the taco shop attached to the Chevron station in Garberville, one of two places in town where Bob felt reasonably secure that no one would spit in his food, the

Mexican workers referred to him as *el chistoso*, "the joker." His favorite place in the world was Disneyland, but he was also a nature lover. He loved the redwoods so much that he swore he'd chain himself to one to keep it from getting chopped down, just as long as he wasn't working that day. A self-professed people person, Bob enjoyed human interaction, even if, as he put it, most of those he interacted with were criminals. "You have to love what you do because you're not doing it for the money," he'd say.

What Bob loved most was helping people.

After four years patrolling Southern Humboldt, it would seem that nothing could surprise Bob anymore, but Humboldt never ceased to deliver. If it wasn't the transients, who were lured there by the pot thing, it was the pot thing itself. Bob viewed Humboldt as one big marijuana haven. Sometimes, when he was driving along in his white department-issued Ford Expedition and the marijuana industry ads came on the radio, they were just so blatant he'd have to reach over and just shut it off, like the one for "Sweet Sticky Fingers," which was supposed to help remove gummy marijuana resin from one's hands.

But then something crazy would happen that would shock Bob out of the silence, those only-in-Humboldt things—like the morning he came across two garbage bags stuffed full of weed in the middle of the highway (they had blown off the back of a truck after a government raid). One time, he saw a man he knew walking toward the bank with massive amounts of cash bulging out of the top of his bag. Another day they got a call at the station from a local motel about a maid who couldn't clean the bathroom in a certain room because it was so full of marijuana. Sure enough, forty pounds of processed pot was found stacked in the shower, on the floor, and on the toilet. Marijuana was literally everywhere in Humboldt County, and Bob was just awaiting the day when he would see starter pot plants for sale next to the trays of baby tomatoes and sunny marigolds the local grocery stores set outside every spring.

Of course Bob knew that marijuana was big business in Humboldt County. He'd spent part of his childhood there, but he'd moved away for many years and didn't really understand what it all meant until he started patrolling the Garberville area in 2006 and noticed all the black garbage bags in the backs of trucks that weren't headed to the dump. It slowly dawned on him that trash bags were what growers used to transport unprocessed marijuana. Then Bob started pulling over people in $40,000 and $50,000 trucks with no visible means of support. Suddenly, the giant pot leaf that towered above the Hemp Connection store on Main Street began to take on a new meaning.

It took Bob a mere month in Southern Humboldt to conclude that America had totally lost the War on Drugs. Everywhere he turned, he'd see that green plant towering above the high fences in people's yards. Every time he confiscated pot from someone he pulled over, he realized it wasn't even a molecule in a drop of water compared to what was out there. What he was doing made no difference at all.

It wasn't easy being a deputy sheriff in a town of outlaws. Just that month, Bob had busted a guy for transporting eighty pounds of pot. Depending on how the pot was grown and which state it was destined for, those eighty pounds were likely worth somewhere between $120,000 and $240,000. The man Bob arrested posted bail and got his truck back that same afternoon. It was what Bob called a "doper diesel" truck, a hulking Ford F-250 or a Dodge Ram, owned by a guy who grows weed indoors with diesel-powered generators. Bob knew the man got out of jail that same day, because he drove by Bob and waved.

"The laws need to be reworked," Bob would say. "We just need to acknowledge that we lost the war on marijuana."

Bob looked forward to the day when he could go into a liquor store and see a pack of Winston Purple Kush next to packs of Salem Sour Diesel and Marlboro Red Hairs. He knew this was a pot grower's greatest fear, the corporatization of the industry, but he'd tell them it was going to be like the microbrewery model versus Anheuser-Busch. Sure, big companies were going to get in on the racket, but they were going to sell leaves, shake, not the primo, high-quality stuff local farmers had spent decades perfecting. In Bob's vision, there would be rolling tobacco–like pouches of Humboldt Gold, full of fat, fragrant buds.

Maybe this would mean that all the growers weren't going to be able to earn a living at it anymore, and people were going to have to get creative and figure out something else to do. He didn't buy the idea that pot was all there was to do in Humboldt. "Think outside the box," Bob would tell people. But they didn't seem to like to hear this much, and sometimes, when Bob was tired of the whole thing, his legalization vision would crumble, and he would just shake his head, sigh, and say, "I am so sick of this pot shit."

Bob had worked his whole life and paid his way and his dues, so it was hard to see locals and people from other states rent property and not report their income. Bob was tired of doing the right thing and watching people get off scot-free. He also had so many other things to deal with, all those other things society needed law enforcement to handle—like domestic violence, child abuse, unlawful dumping, burglaries, and reckless driving. The weird thing was, when the home invasion robberies happened, Bob often ended up protecting the growers from the outside man.

Recently, Bob had shared his frustrations with a reporter for the *Los Angeles Times*. The story, "In Humboldt County, Deputies' Jobs Can Get a Little Hazy," earned Bob a lot of grief in the coastal town of Shelter Cove, where he lived part time. He had already recently both amused and annoyed some people by playing a joke and showing up to a community fund-raiser with confiscated pot plants tied to the top and bumper of his sheriff's SUV like some kind of hunting trophy. After the article appeared, people in the Cove had T-shirts printed that read, "Don't Be the Local Bob," with multiple sets of nosy eyes peering out on the front. On the back, they read, "& Burst Our Bubble." One of Bob's points in the article was that not all dope growers with medical cards were growing only for their pain management, and that most, if not all, were growing for the black market.

Back on the bluff, as the angry sound of a chain saw

roared to life, one of the men in charge of the inmate crew checked with Sergeant Kenny Swithenbank to see if they should cut down the oak trees that were scattered among the brush.

"Naw, leave 'em," Kenny instructed.

With the brush clearing under way, the sheriff's deputies set out to check on another homeless encampment down by the river. Bob followed Kenny in a two-car convoy down a steep road toward the river bar, a wide strip of rocks that covered the banks of the South Fork of the Eel River. As they passed under Bear Canyon Bridge, the overpass that separates Garberville from Redway, a man standing by the river next to a white sedan exhaled a giant cloud of smoke into the air.

Before the smoke had a chance to dissipate, both deputies hit their lights and bounded out of their SUVs. While Bob frisked the smoker, and the two men who had been sitting in the car next to him, Kenny ran their names through dispatch to see if there were any warrants out for their arrest.

"And the Meek Shall Inherit the Earth" was spray-painted on a concrete block a few feet away from where Bob patted down the men. Next to that, someone had written, somewhat less profoundly, in pink paint, "Go Hippies."

The smoker, it turned out, had not been hitting a crack pipe, as the deputies had suspected. He had taken a hit of pot from a pipe he had stuffed into a sock and hidden among the rocks. Since there were no outstanding warrants, Kenny and Bob left the smokers by their car and continued back down the river bar, the rocks crunching noisily under their tires.

About half a mile downriver, they pulled to a stop. Bob led the way through the bushes to a trail that was lined neatly with river stones. It wound past a bed of purple pansies, a few tomato plants, and a hand-painted "Welcome" sign, to a clearing where large tarps were strung up over pop-up tents. Two men were sitting in chairs there sipping coffee. The younger of the two had long red hair. His companion had a white beard and wore a red knit cap.

"Good morning," Kenny Swithenbank said. "Do you know whose property you're on?

"No," the older man said, "but we're trying to be respectful."

A large Alaskan husky bounded up to Bob, and he reached down and gave it a pat. It smelled of clean, warm fur. Names were established. Rob was the older gentleman in the cap. Zach was twenty-two and from Colorado.

There was the sound of a zipper opening, and a young woman emerged from one of the tents, leaving a dozen puppies yipping in her wake. Her name was Jessica. She had strawberry blond hair and looked like she could be Zach's sister. She was wearing sweatpants and a sheer tank top that clung tightly to her eight-months-pregnant belly. She began to roll a cigarette.

"Why'd you come out here from Colorado?" Kenny asked Zach. "Marijuana maybe?"

"Marijuana is my medicine," Zach replied.

"Really?" Bob asked. "Why are you sick?"

Zach ignored him.

"Why did you come here?" Kenny pressed in a calm voice.

Zach rambled about having heard about the redwoods, and then he conceded, "I heard there was good herb out here and jobs to trim."

"Did you find a job?" asked Kenny.

"No, but I've met a lot of friendly people."

Rob, with the red cap, interjected: "Are you kidding? The Humboldt scene is so popular, I tell people to stay away. The jobs aren't happening because the growers go and get sixty-year-old women, or they go to Arcata and get some hot college girls."

"It's their million-dollar business and they aren't going to trust strangers with it," Kenny said knowingly. He then asked Zach what his home life was like.

"When I was little my mom sold pot to support us," Zach said.

Jessica took a drag off her cigarette, seemingly oblivious to the conversation unfolding in front of her.

"When I was here in June, this place was the shit," she said. "The Veterans Park was open. The weather was better."

While Jessica was talking, Bob slipped into the bushes nearby to make a phone call. When he returned, he pulled a pair of handcuffs off his belt.

"Please stand up," he instructed Rob, who, it turned out, was wanted on a five-year-old warrant for a parole violation in Virginia.

Bob clicked the handcuffs onto Rob's wrists, and Zach

held a thermos up to his friend's lips so he could have one last sip of coffee before he was hauled off to jail.

As he turned to go, Kenny looked thoughtful.

"I'm not sure who the property owner is—I think it is my cousin's—but you guys need to think about leaving. I appreciate your respect here, but you are trespassing, and I guarantee that the owner doesn't want you here. All the homeless camps in Southern Humboldt are on private property."

Back at his truck, Bob loaded Rob into the back and shut the door. It was over an hour's drive to Eureka, the county seat, and the nearest holding tank. From the passenger seat, Bob pulled out an enormous green T-shirt and held it up against his chest. It was the T-shirt someone had made up in Shelter Cove after the *L.A. Times* article came out.

"Don't Be the Local Bob," it read.

Bob grinned, but he seemed a little perplexed. "All I did was tell the truth," he said, shaking his head, which was that he was fed up with working in a gray area and wished the government would either totally ban marijuana or make it totally legal, but no more of this in-between stuff.

Behind him, on a bluff in the distance, a thick black plume of burning brush curled into the air. On days like this, it was hard to imagine that there was once a time in Humboldt County when pot wasn't everywhere.

CHAPTER FIVE

Mare

Late one morning in the winter of 1970, when Mare
Abidon was a young woman of thirty, with blond hair
that streamed down her back, she stood outside her San
Francisco apartment holding a cardboard box and prepared
to say good-bye. The box in her arms brimmed with the remnants of the life she was leaving behind, and all the lives
that came before that: art supplies from school, horn jewelry
purchased on the street in India, and batik granny dresses
from her years in the Haight. Len was waiting in his truck
nearby. Brooding Len with the dark beard and strong arms,
who had made Mare's heart skip a beat the first time she
laid eyes on him years ago at the post office.

Instead of feeling melancholy about the life she was
leaving behind, Mare was brimming with excitement. The
Beast, Len's old green Chevy, was loaded down with their
belongings and ready to carry them north.

Six years earlier, Mare had arrived in San Francisco with

her new husband, Gene. When her marriage fell apart a year later, she fled to the Haight-Ashbury. What a refuge the Haight had been. The neighborhood was brimming with creativity and hope. The Grateful Dead, Janis Joplin, and Jefferson Airplane all called it home. The Diggers served free soup down the Panhandle from Mare's apartment. The Haight was famous the world over. During that summer they called Love, even more dreamers flocked to San Francisco. There was such a spirit of freedom and communalism to the place that, for a moment, Mare really believed love could conquer all.

But then things took a darker turn. Some of Mare's friends started shooting heroin. A severed arm was found in the back of a car in the neighborhood, and hate began creeping in. Early one morning, when Mare was walking back from her graveyard shift at the post office, someone in a passing car screamed out the window at her:

"Get a job!"

Oh, leave me alone, Mare thought. I have two.

In addition to working the night shift at the post office to pay the bills, by day, she was an art student. What had started out as a way to find herself and gain some confidence years ago in Michigan had evolved into a full-blown passion. Mare honed her painting and sculpture skills with classes at San Francisco State and the University of California at Berkeley.

It had slowly dawned on Mare that she wasn't the kind of person who could work and do her art on the side. Then one of her Berkeley professors made it clear that this was a futile endeavor anyway.

"Female artists should find husbands to subsidize their careers; professorships are for men," she had overheard him telling another female student.

As those words sank into her, Mare's dreams crashed and burned.

Then, one afternoon after class, as Mare stood on the sidewalk waiting for the bus, a car pulled up alongside her. The man inside offered her a lift.

"No, brother, I don't need a ride," she told him.

But the man had a gun, and forced her inside the car. He proceeded to drive to a desolate place. Mare kept thinking she could talk her way out of what happened next, but she couldn't, and he raped her.

Nothing made sense anymore. For all these reasons and more, it seemed like a good time to start over someplace far from civilization and its discontents.

Mare took one last look at the building on Twentieth Avenue in San Francisco's fog-shrouded Sunset District, then carried her box to the truck and never looked back. The plan was to head north, past Marin and Sonoma, to the place where the counties of Mendocino and Humboldt meet. Some of Len's buddies from high school had started a commune at an old lumber camp there. They called it Gopherville.

The idea to move there came to Mare and Len a few months earlier, at the end of summer, after they had helped Mare's cousin Jewel and her husband build a house in the Humboldt Hills. Mare had fallen in love with the big trees, and she wondered what it would be like to pass through them every day on the way home. On the way back to the city that summer, she and Len had stopped off near the coast at Gopherville.

As Mare and Len looked around at the various buildings set back in the trees, and the seemingly tranquil life they provided, Len's old friend Bob pointed to a house on the hill. A family had just moved out. It was theirs if they wanted it. They did.

With their decision to leave the city and start anew, Mare and Len joined a wave of young people who were fleeing urban America at the time. With *Whole Earth Catalogs* and *Mother Earth News* magazines in hand, these idealist youth were leaving behind the "American Dream" and its tarnished illusions of material wealth and success. They headed into the countryside of Northern California, upstate New York, Vermont, and elsewhere to grow their own food, live simply, and be self-sufficient. It was one of America's last great pioneer movements. It was known as Back-to-the-Land.

All Mare knew was that, in the words of Joseph Campbell, she was going to follow her bliss, to live as an artist and be free. In a way, the quest for freedom had been driving her ever since she was old enough to determine her own destiny. Mary Em Abidon was born in Chicago in 1940, just before America entered the Second World War. Her parents, Walker and Lola Belle, had met a few years earlier, at the University of Wisconsin, where Lola Belle earned a master's in nutrition and Walker studied the classics. Lola Belle was the first woman from her Wisconsin town to attend college. Walker hailed from a family of southern physicians, and became a doctor of philosophy. When Mare was two, her parents returned home from the hospital with a freshly swaddled newborn. At first, Mare thought her baby sister, Ellen, was a doll they'd bought for her to play with.

The Abidons eventually settled in East Lansing, Michigan, where Walker taught at the local university and Lola Belle focused on being a housewife. Like so many women of her generation, Lola Belle believed being a good mother meant staying at home and devoting herself to her family. Mare watched her mother give up all her hopes, dreams, and ambition for family life, and even though Lola Belle excelled at it, Mare knew it wasn't all her mother wanted. Mare also knew it wasn't all *she* wanted, either. Like many a daughter, Mare looked at the decisions of her mother and ran in the opposite direction.

Mare's rebellion began in earnest during her junior year of high school, when the family moved to India for the year and Mare began going for long motorbike rides in the countryside with a male friend. Later, at Antioch College in Ohio, Mare wore dark turtlenecks and heavy eyeliner and emulated the Beats. During her junior semester abroad, in Mexico, she discovered the heady calm of marijuana. Then she dropped out of college and headed back to India for a few years to teach. She met her first and only husband, Gene, there. He was a Peace Corps doctor, and they moved to San Francisco together. Gene had wanted her to be a good housewife and to obey.

"Only one person can make the decisions," he told her.

Then he started taking her to Ronald Reagan for Governor fund-raisers. The marriage lasted less than a year. Mare met Len shortly thereafter. He had caught her eye on the first day of work at the post office. Two other girls at work were also crazy about him, but Mare won the right to flirt with him in a coin toss. Mare and Len later married themselves in an unofficial ceremony in Golden Gate Park.

As the heavily loaded-down Chevy headed north on Highway 101 that winter afternoon, Mare felt giddy. She was finally doing it: she was breaking free. When the Beast passed through that ancient patch of redwoods called Richardson Grove, Mare thought to herself, Oh good, now I'll get to pass through these trees on my way home. Little did she know that she would one day risk her life to protect them.

As the Beast emerged from the grove, the mountains ahead were awash with green. It was as if someone had drawn them in oil pastel and delicately smudged the edges. As they grew closer, the pointy tops of every individual tree came into focus, the redwoods tall and skinny like candlesticks, and the Douglas firs fuller, like Christmas trees. It was the kind of landscape upon which dreams are built, and one that had attracted outlaws, rebels, fortune seekers, and dreamers for as long as white men had been coming west.

———

Shaped like a long, slender piece of a jigsaw puzzle, Humboldt County is located on the far northern coast of California. Its immediate neighbor to the south is the county of Mendocino; to the east, Trinity and Siskiyou; and to the north, Del Norte. The frigid waters of the Pacific Ocean crash into Humboldt's western shore. The county's terrain ranges from sea level at the coast to 6,000 feet along its eastern edge. Much of its 3,600 square miles are covered in dense forest. In April 1850, the crew from a ship called the *Laura Virginia* christened the large bay near what would become known as Eureka in honor of the famous German naturalist and explorer Alexander von Humboldt, a man who never visited the place but was fond of botany and surely would have loved it. The county was named after its bay.

Humboldt's first town was established soon thereafter. The pioneer population grew throughout the 1850s, during the gold mining boom in neighboring Trinity County. Businessmen viewed Humboldt's seaport as a way to get supplies overland from San Francisco to the men in the mines. Then red gold was discovered.

The story of the people who called the place home for thousands of years prior is a tragically familiar one. The arrival of pioneers spelled death and displacement for the Wiyot, Yurok, Hupa, Karuk, and Sinkyone peoples, among others. In one particularly grisly attack, known as the Wiyot Massacre, on February 26, 1860, white settlers murdered somewhere between 80 and 250 Wiyot men, women, and children. Writer Bret Harte detailed the carnage in the *Northern Californian* newspaper: "Blood stood in pools on all sides; the walls of the huts were stained and the grass colored red."

By 1881, twenty-two sawmills were ripping through redwoods across the county, and men were pouring in to work at them. In the black-and-white photographs from the time, the loggers look like Lilliputians standing next to downed giants. Mills buzzed from Oregon to Big Sur as the century turned, and the ancient trees were felled at a rapid rate. In 1874, Walt Whitman composed an ode to their death called "Song of the Redwood Tree."

> *Murmuring out of its myriad leaves,*
> *Down from its lofty top rising two hundred feet*
> *   high,*
> *Out of its stalwart trunk and limbs, out of its foot-*
> *   thick bark,*
> *That chant of the seasons and time, chant not of*
> *   the past only but the future.*

In 1917, the head of the National Park Service sent three men to investigate the state of Northern California's redwood forests. When the men reached the Bull Creek–Dyerville Flat area in Humboldt County, they were so in awe of the three-hundred-foot-tall trees they saw there, legend has it they took off their hats and spoke in hushed tones. Within a year, the men founded Save the Redwoods League, to help preserve the last of the virgin redwood forest for future generations.

By the time Mare Abidon arrived in Humboldt County at the end of 1970, the timber industry had slowed to a dull rumble. The land was heavily logged, setting the stage for a later showdown over the fate of the few giants that were left standing. Much of this logged land was considered worthless by ranchers and loggers, and was sold cheaply.

Into this landscape arrived the idealistic, young "new people," as those who were there before called them. They puttered into town in Volkswagen Beetles, school buses with flowers painted on the sides, and old Chevy trucks with nicknames. They looked around and thought they had found paradise. There were no massacres following this new wave of settlers, only hostility and cultural misunderstandings. The new people settled on remote tracts of land with no electricity or plumbing. Some places were so difficult to access they had to be hiked into. The new people had no real income. Many were on welfare. The old-timers wondered how they'd survive, these kids who'd grown up in cities, who reeked of scented oils and swam naked in the Eel River. This first wave of new settlers—the ones who came to Humboldt before it became synonymous with its clandestine crop—would, in later times, promptly remind people that they hadn't moved there to grow pot. They'd come to be righteous and free. What happened next was Manifest Destiny.

As the Beast and its passengers continued on their journey that afternoon, they passed Garberville and Redway, the two hamlets that everyone referred to collectively as "town," and hung a left on the Briceland–Shelter Cove Road. After veering right at an intersection known as Whitethorn Junction, they drove into Whitethorn proper, which seemed straight out of an old Western. In those days, Whitethorn consisted of not much more than Mrs. Marker's general store and an enormous redwood stump that the young men who had just returned from Vietnam would gather around to dull their memories with booze and darker things.

Gopherville was set back in the woods down the road. At its height, about twenty adults and six children lived on the commune, in cabins that had once housed millworkers. One building had been turned into a family house, where everyone gathered to eat dinner together around an enormous redwood table.

Looking back, Mare would recall her years at Gopherville as the happiest time of her life. It was, she would say, the closest she ever came to Nirvana. Len gathered wood and chased away rabid skunks, while Mare focused on her art. One day she stumbled across a ceramics kit in the commune dump. She set it up in an old chicken coop and started playing with clay, moving her hands over the moist earth, coaxing it gently into shape.

Mare also loved to spend time in the commune's garden, where they grew vegetables and a little marijuana in raised beds. Pot was a popular drug among the counterculture, of course, and the Back-to-the-Landers discovered that, just as they could grow their own tomatoes, they could pick the seeds out of pot they bought and sow them in the ground. A few of the mothers who lived on the commune were on welfare and would share their government checks, which, along with the vegetables from the garden, helped sustain everyone. Pot wasn't worth much in those days; once, Mare traded some for enough gas to get her to the city. Mostly, though, marijuana was just something the new people grew for their own pleasure.

Time passed in a blur at Gopherville, the way it does when one is happy. So it came as quite a shock when Mare learned that not everyone on the commune felt the same way she did, and it all came screeching to a halt.

All along the North Coast, experiments in communal living flickered out in various ways, but the beginning of the end of Gopherville can be traced to a trip a couple of commune members made to a place called Lighthouse Ranch. Located at an old Coast Guard station in the north of the county, Lighthouse Ranch was a religious commune owned by a real estate agent and evangelical Christian minister named Jim Durkin. Brother Durkin gave Mare the creeps. He reminded her of Willy Loman from *Death of a Salesman*. She found him overbearing, paunchy, and slobbering. Her unfavorable view stemmed in part from what happened next: the two commune members who visited Lighthouse Ranch returned to Gopherville and, one by one, began converting others into what Mare could only describe as dreary Jesus freaks. Those who didn't convert had to leave.

Mare was heartbroken. It felt as though her family were breaking apart. At one point, one of her recently converted sisters came to her in her clay studio/chicken coop and suggested that Mare ask Jesus into her heart.

"Just try," the woman coaxed her. "Invite him in and see what happens."

Mare knelt on the floor of her studio and asked Jesus into her heart.

He didn't make an appearance.

Mare hung around a bit longer, but the breaking point

came when Brother Durkin sent word that she was forbidden from working in the garden and that a woman's place was in the kitchen.

"Bullshit" was her response.

Len had also had enough of the new Gopherville by then. Mare and Len left the commune and camped nearby, on the Mattole River, for a while. Over time their interests diverged, and the couple saw less of each other. Mare spent the following years camping in the summer and caretaking homes in the winter. She joined a woman's consciousness-raising group, where she forged close friendships, and made ends meet selling pottery at the annual Bay Area Renaissance fair. Somewhere in the middle of it all, something happened that changed the economy of the area. When Mare heard about it, she thought it was exciting. It was a new horticultural technique that produced marijuana that was so potent people in the cities were willing to pay a lot of money for it.

It was called *sinsemilla*.

It's difficult to pinpoint the exact moment when the technique for growing sinsemilla, or seedless pot, arrived in Humboldt County, but it was most likely sometime around 1974 or 1975. Mare thought she heard about it from the Vietnam veterans. Others recall a man who passed through town and instructed everyone to "pull all the males." One thing is for sure, word spread fast, and soon everyone was growing what the media would soon come to call "the Cadillac of cannabis." Sinsemilla may have been born elsewhere, but Humboldt growers mastered it.

Marijuana, which is Mexican slang for cannabis, is a

flowering annual. All species of cannabis are dioecious—that is, male and female flowers appear on separate plants. Males produce pollen, and females produce seeds—and that's where the trickery begins. Both plants produce flowers, but unpollinated females produce much more resin, the sticky substance that contains both the terpenes that give pot its potent aroma and the cannabinoids that are responsible for its psychoactive properties, notably delta-9-tetrahydrocannabinol, or THC. In order to grow seedless female flowers, sinsemilla, you must remove the male plants before pollination.

Around the same time that marijuana growers in Humboldt and the neighboring counties of Trinity and Mendocino began producing sinsemilla, the U.S. government inadvertently helped create a market for their new industry. In the mid- to late 1970s, the American government supported the Mexican government's spraying of the toxic herbicide paraquat on the Mexican marijuana crop. At the time, more than 90 percent of the marijuana smoked in the United States came from abroad. The strains were called Acapulco Gold, Colombian Gold, and Panama Red, after the places where they were grown. Like the jug wines that graced American dinner tables at the time, these were simple, lightweight versions of what was to come.

Marijuana continued to flow north from Mexico, but after the Centers for Disease Control and Prevention (CDC) warned of the serious health risks that paraquat-laced pot posed to consumers, there was a sudden interest in other sources. By 1979, the year Congress suspended the paraquat-spraying program, an estimated 35 percent of the marijuana smoked in California was homegrown. This percentage would only continue to rise in the following years, as California marijuana became synonymous around the state and nation with a quality high. By 2010, the year of the legalization vote, one study estimated that 79 percent of all marijuana consumed in the United States came from California.

And so an industry was born in Humboldt County, one that would bridge the cultural divide between hippies and rednecks by providing income for all, and would bring a new economic boom to the area just as the old industries were drying up. Word spread, and people flocked from faraway places to cash in. As the pillar of the local economy became a forbidden plant, Mare would hear stories about friends who had helped teach old-timers how to grow. On her trips into town, she'd notice how some hippies had started wearing the checked flannel shirts of the loggers, and how some of the rednecks had begun wearing their hair long. Things started to feel more equal. The children of the two cultures were the true hybrids. They went to school together, became friends, and fell in love with each other. As the local logging and fishing industries dwindled even further, bumper stickers began to appear on the backs of the dusty pickups around town announcing the transition: "Another Logger Gone to Pot."

By 1979, even *The New York Times* took note. "Marijuana Crops Revived California Town" was the headline of an article about Garberville. The story was one that would be retold in every medium over the coming decades: growers had made a killing with their latest harvest ("$500 to $1000 a pound, five to 10 times the price paid five years ago"); Main Street was bustling; sheriff's deputies had confiscated more pot than the year before; and there had been an uptick in marijuana-related crime. Accompanying the article were photos of deputies standing next to long, leafy plants that, to the untrained eye, looked like freshly cut bamboo.

Perhaps the case that best represents how pervasive marijuana growing became in Humboldt County over the years, how it transcended social and class boundaries until seemingly everyone was doing it, is the story of the lieutenant sheriff's deputy Delbert Frame. Del Frame, as he was known, grew up on a dairy farm in Ferndale. He was a tall man with a round, Nordic face and blond hair that he wore combed neatly back. He'd met his wife, Rita, at Boston University and had fought in the Korean War. The couple had three sons and a daughter, and they eventually settled in a ranch-style home on Sunset Avenue in Redway. Del Frame ran the Garberville sheriff's substation in the 1970s, where he was remembered as a kind and calm boss. Rita worked as a court clerk.

After his retirement, when Del Frame was sixty and recovering from his third heart attack at a hospital three hours south, law enforcement broke down his front door. Many of the men who took part in the raid that day had been to the house before as guests. A neighbor had tipped off the authorities that Del Frame, veteran, dairyman, and, most important, retired lieutenant sheriff's deputy, was growing marijuana on land he owned up Alderpoint Road.

"Everybody else is doing it, why not us?" Frame had told his wife before he planted his first crop. Rita Frame didn't think it was such a good idea, but Del was always so confident. He didn't seem to have a problem with people smoking pot, either, as long as they didn't abuse it. The Frames always thought alcohol was worse. Besides, the extra money would help their kids get ahead in the world.

Authorities seized more than four hundred pot plants from Del Frame's property on the hill. His partner in the operation, a former highway patrolman named Bud Miller, was also arrested. Frame was tried, and sentenced to five years in federal prison. Two months after his release, he had a stroke while sitting in an easy chair in his living room on Sunset Avenue. He died six years later.

Mare, meanwhile, continued to help Len grow a little marijuana down by the river. She earned most of her income, however, selling clay pots at the Renaissance fair. She didn't really start growing her own crop until 1980, after her father loaned her the money to buy her land. That was just before the dull, sickening sound of helicopters moving through the sky became commonplace every fall. The War on Drugs played out in a different way in the hills of Humboldt than it did in the inner city and beyond the southern border. Prices skyrocketed as the stakes were raised, and the unlucky experienced the devastation and stigma of being busted.

CHAPTER SIX

Emma

The day the sheriff came began like any other. That September morning in 1997, Sage woke Emma Worldpeace and her sister Lisa in the bedroom they shared at Morning Glory Manor. She brewed a pot of coffee while the girls brushed their hair and washed the sleep from their eyes. Their older siblings, Aia and Omar, walked up to the house from the barn, and everyone ate breakfast together and packed a quick lunch before it was time to pile into the Pathfinder and drive to Ettersburg Junction to meet the school bus.

As usual, Emma was nervous about missing the bus and was the first inside the car.

"Hurry up!" she shouted. "We're going to be late!!"

The bus ride to school was only around fifteen miles, but the journey took close to an hour, due to all the stops to pick up other students and the bumpy, unpaved road that forced them to move at a crawl.

The tiny alternative school that Emma and her siblings attended was perched on a bluff near the coast. The school year began with a field trip so the students could get to know one another. There were group meditation classes, and a choice between aikido and African dance for P.E. Years earlier an artist named Mare used to teach the students how to make paper and clay faces.

Emma's older sister, Aia, had a dentist appointment that morning and stayed home from school, but everyone else made it to the bus on time. Nothing really remarkable happened that morning, until Emma's teacher pulled her aside.

"There's something going on at your house," she said. "Your mom doesn't want you to take the bus all the way home."

Normally, the bus would drop Emma off at the top of her driveway. On this day, Emma, Omar, and Lisa were instructed to get off at Ettersburg Junction. When they pulled up, Sage was standing in front of the Pathfinder with baby John on her hip. Aia was sitting in the passenger seat. Sage looked like a ghost. It was clear that she had been crying and was trying to hold it together.

It was obvious that something horrible had happened.

A few days earlier, a black helicopter had buzzed Morning Glory Manor. As everyone knew, a helicopter flying low across Southern Humboldt at the time was usually looking for only one thing. In the fall of 1983, the ominous sound of helicopter blades cutting through the air became common-place at harvest time. It echoed up and down valleys and gulches, and made stomachs cramp and heart rates acceler-ate among those who grew illegal plants, for it signaled the arrival of the Campaign Against Marijuana Planting.

CAMP, as it was commonly known, was a task force of federal, state, and local agencies operated by the Califor-nia Department of Justice's Bureau of Narcotic Enforce-ment. On any given day during the eight-week-long CAMP season, members of various agencies, including the Drug Enforcement Agency, the Department of Fish and Game, the Coast Guard, local sheriff's deputies, and others, would participate in a very involved version of weed whacking. Only they didn't call it weed; they called it dope.

Law enforcement had been chopping down marijuana in Humboldt—eradicating, as they called it—since a sheriff's deputy arrested Eugene Crawford next to his tiny plants back in 1960. Starting with Operation Sinsemilla in 1979, federal and state funds helped eradication efforts become larger and more militarized. CAMP helicopters were filled with men prepared for battle: dressed in camouflage and armed with automatic weapons.

To growers, helicopters were the ultimate crop-destroying locusts.

After spotting and photographing marijuana grows from the air, authorities would return on raids. Pot would be chopped down, hauled out, and burned or buried. When-ever possible, the grower was arrested. The annual raids led to the creation of a term among growers: to get

"CAMP'ed" meant that law enforcement had destroyed your garden. In the 1980s and throughout the '90s, the era before medical marijuana, there was more focus on small-time pot growers, and anyone could get CAMP'ed. As the helicopters swarmed the hills for weeks on end, it was like a game of *Dungeons & Dragons*. As one longtime grower described it, "You never knew where the dice were going to land."

The greenhouse that contained the plants Sage was growing that season was located next to the barn. It was usually covered in plastic sheeting. The day the helicopter passed over, Roland, the man who was helping Sage grow her crop that year, had peeled back the plastic because the plants were growing tall and pushing up against it. Sage and Roland had planned to go down to Whitethorn Construction that day to get poles to make the greenhouse taller, but before they left, the helicopter swooped over the ridgetop.

"Oh my God, Roland!" Sage yelled. "Cover it!"

But it was too late.

The helicopter passed overhead with a clear view of thirty tall green plants flourishing inside the open greenhouse.

Everyone in the family felt a little nervous afterward, but Sage decided not to cut the plants down. They weren't yet ready for harvest. She knew it was a risk, leaving them there for law enforcement to confiscate, but before giving the matter any more thought, a friend's five-year-old child died in a horrible car accident. Sage became so preoccupied with her friend's grief that she forgot all about the helicopter and the risk she was taking leaving her plants in the ground—

until she pulled up at her house with Aia on the way back from the dentist that morning.

The gate was open.

"That's weird," Aia remarked. "Didn't we leave the gate closed?"

Then Sage and Aia noticed the strange cars parked next to the barn. There was a jeep, a green truck, and another vehicle they had never seen before. They were confused. By the time they figured out what was going on, they had been spotted.

"Are you Linda Looney?" one of the CAMP officers asked Sage after she rolled down her window.

"No," Sage replied, truthfully.

Later, they would learn that CAMP had pulled the name off a school paper in Aia's bedroom.

"Then you can turn around and leave if you want."

But Sage didn't leave. Baby John, in the backseat, was tired and in need of changing.

"I need to go up to my house and get some diapers for my baby," she said.

Sage also demanded to see a search warrant. There was an affidavit for a search warrant. Sage and Aia sat in the living room while officials from CAMP searched the house and grounds.

When Emma got home after school, she discovered that Morning Glory Manor had been turned upside down. It was like a scene from a movie where someone discovers their house has been ransacked. All the closets were open, and every box and bag that had been inside them was piled on the floor. Sage's bedroom was the worst of all. All her drawers were open, and most of their contents had been dumped on her bed. The crib where baby John slept was upturned. In Aia's room, in the barn, her bed had been thrown against the wall, and shards of a smashed mirror littered the ground. In Emma and Lisa's bedroom, the cabinets were open, and clothing was strewn across the floor. Most embarrassing for Emma was that someone had gone through her underwear drawer, found her memory box, and dug through its contents. She had been collecting keepsakes in the old shoebox—letters from boys she liked, ticket stubs from movies, and all the other little things that document a budding life.

When the authorities left, they handed over a list of everything they were taking with them. It included Aia's passport, a small amount of cash from Omar's room, and photos from the family albums that included images of the three girls. In one, they smiled at the camera from the kitchen table, with marijuana branches hanging from the rafters behind them. In another, they sat at the same table industriously clipping pot. Most devastating of all, authorities seized the cash they'd found under Sage's bed, which had been set aside to cover the mortgage over the coming year. Sage would eventually be charged with marijuana cultivation, possession, intent to sell, and child endangerment.

For ten-year-old Emma, the bust was a life-changing event. It was traumatic. Things got hard fast. The money taken from under Sage's bed had been her mother's entire savings. The plants that would have sustained the family through another year were also gone. Sage signed up for food stamps. There were trips to the food bank, and lots of cheap polenta dinners. During the long months that followed, there were many long drives north to Eureka for court appearances. Emma would push John in his stroller down the long courthouse hallways while her mother met with lawyers and a judge. Emma felt ashamed about what had happened, and didn't feel like she could talk about it with her friends at school. The strangling code of secrecy extended even to busts.

Sage tried to fight the charges—she didn't want a felony on her record—but in the end, she took a plea bargain and was sentenced to three years' probation and community service, which she spent working at the Garberville thrift store. With no money to make her land payments, she eventually had to sell Morning Glory Manor. Around the same time, she also discovered, at the age of forty-two, that she was pregnant with her sixth child. So she gathered up her children and moved in with her partner, Jim. It was close quarters. Emma, Lisa, and Aia slept in a queen-size bed, and Omar on a futon in the downstairs living room. Jim's son Mike had already left home around this time. He had dropped out of high school at age sixteen and moved in with an overweight Filipino named Robert Juan, whom everyone called Buddha. Years later, Buddha would go down in one of the biggest busts in Southern Humboldt history, but at the time, he was a prosperous pot grower, and Mike lived in a shed on his property. Emma would see Mike when she went up to trim pot for Buddha. Like many girls in her community, Emma had begun trimming pot for pocket money at an early age, about thirteen.

Once, while Emma was living with her mom and Jim, Mike's older brother, Shadrach, came to visit. Mike's mother had left when he was just a toddler; Shadrach was her son from another relationship. The day he called round to the house looking for Mike, Emma couldn't help but notice the massive tattoos that covered Shadrach's arms and the slash mark–shaped scars across his chest.

He told her the scars were from where he had been stabbed.

Shadrach's face looked weathered and old, and he seemed spun out on drugs, and dangerous. As he sat on the couch in the living room next to her little brother, John, all Emma's instincts screamed at her to get the baby away from him.

On that same visit, Shadrach sealed his fate in the community. It was close to harvest, and Emma had heard that he had ripped some people off. Some local teenagers had found Shadrach in an abandoned cabin in the hills, high on heroin and surrounded by trash bags full of stolen weed. He was last seen leaving town on a Greyhound bus.

Later, Shadrach became a legend when a local group known as the Camo Cowboys released an album about marijuana culture, including the songs "Family Felony," about the multigenerational nature of the business, and "Flower Police," about how the cops who bust growers kept the prices high. Included on the album was a melancholy tune called "The Ballad of Shadrack."

Oh Shadrach. Just a broken boy.
Cast aside by your mama, just like a broken toy.
Oh Shadrach, just a thieving punk.
Your bridges are all burned and all your ships are
*   sunk.*
Every fall when the plants were tall,
you'd come creeping in
and rip off your neighbors again and again and
*   again.*
Oh Shadrach, just a broken boy.
Cast aside by your mama just like a broken toy.

At the end of the song, Shadrach overdoses in Santa Cruz. In reality, Shadrach ended up in prison. When the song came out, Emma caught Mike listening to it over and over again. She didn't understand how he could handle it; the song was so damned sad. In a way, Mike's mother had cast him aside like a broken toy, too. Emma met her once when she came back to visit. She showed up at Jim's house in a stolen U-Haul and announced that there was a man in the back of the truck who was dying of AIDS. She had a young boy with her, another son. All of them looked like they were dying to Emma. It must have been the only time in Mike's memory that he saw his mother. There was screaming and yelling. Emma retreated upstairs. She could hear Jim chasing Mike's mother off and telling her never to come back.

Around this same time, Emma quit smoking pot. She was thirteen years old. She was at her friend Anika's house, and the two girls had been lying on bunk beds getting high. Anika's mother came in and noticed the smell. She was not one of the more permissive parents.

"What are you doing, little girls?" she asked. "That's not cool, you can't be smoking pot."

Something about her words stuck, and Emma and Anika decided then and there that pot smoking wasn't so cool, and that they weren't going to smoke anymore. To solidify their intention, the girls decided to destroy their stash. They did so in a very Humboldt way. Whereas the rest of America might have flushed the pot down the toilet, in a region short on indoor plumbing, the girls did the next best thing. They knelt on the banks of a nearby creek and dumped the contents of their plastic baggie into the rushing water and quietly watched the dried green flowers float away.

The decision to stop smoking pot would help Emma focus more on her studies. It would also allow her to see clearly that something was wrong in Humboldt when her friends started dying.

The feeling of being in danger, of being unsafe, didn't begin until Emma Worldpeace started high school. Emma was a bookworm growing up and was often immersed in a story. She especially loved to read memoirs and novels about other people's childhoods. Dorothy Allison's *Bastard Out of Carolina* left quite an impression on her. The story of incest and abuse made Emma feel all the more that there was something idyllic about her community. Sure, things were a little weird because people grew pot and you weren't supposed to talk about it, but Southern Humboldt felt like a safe place. Emma could run around naked, and her parents, whatever their shortcomings, had always been so idealistic and hippie, and there were always plenty of hugs and a lot of love to go around.

In the beginning of her freshman year, in 2001, Emma started going to parties up dirt roads in the middle of nowhere. People would get wasted—snort coke, do ecstasy—and no one would have a designated driver. Fights would break out, things felt messy and out of control, and Emma started thinking that maybe something was wrong. People didn't seem to be taking care of themselves. It was like they lived in a world without boundaries, and since teenagers needed something to push against, it didn't become obvious that things were going too far until people starting falling over the edge.

Soon, what Emma would come to call the "sad-ass stories" began.

Throughout her childhood, Emma's brother Omar's best friend was a boy named Sean Akselsen. Sean had dark brown hair and blue-green eyes. He grew into a handsome young man whom many girls developed crushes on, but in Emma's mind, he remained the twelve-year-old boy who liked to skate and draw, and who practiced backflips in the backyard. Sean Akselsen spent a lot of time over the years hanging out at Morning Glory Manor, and Emma loved him. His chuckle was infectious. They rode the school bus together in elementary school, and would listen to Tom Petty and sing the lyrics to "You Don't Know How It Feels," singing especially loud to the line that had particular resonance in their community: "But let me get to the point, let's roll another joint."

In the summer months, Emma would often join Omar, Sean, and two brothers everyone called the Twin Rats, and they'd trudge off down a dirt road to the Whitethorn Junction swimming hole—the junction hole, as they called it. It was a beautiful spot, surrounded by shade trees. A sun-bleached rope hung from one of the trees, and they could swing out on it and plunge into the deep, cool water below.

One day in his high school art class, Sean Akselsen designed a T-shirt that read, "Whitethorn Riders. Got Gas?" above the image of a car. The shirt was a hit, and everyone wanted one. Sean, Omar, and their friends started calling themselves the Whitethorn Riders. In her freshman year, Emma briefly dated a Whitethorn Rider named Kaleb Garza. Kaleb was a senior who drove a souped-up Toyota Celica. He took Emma to the prom in a black tuxedo with a burgundy bow tie. She wore a pale green dress.

The first sad-ass story occurred at the beginning of Emma's junior year of high school. On August 25, 2003, Sean Akselsen, the boy Emma used to sing along with to Tom Petty, who used to do backflips in her yard, was murdered in a pot deal. Akselsen wasn't the first youth from the community to be killed for his involvement in the industry. Ten years earlier, in August 1993, a twenty-year-old named John Wyatt Jameton was shot in the head and left to die in the middle of a gravel road during a deal gone wrong. The basic details of Sean Akselsen's murder were eerily similar.

Emma heard that Sean Akselsen had agreed to sell a pound of pot to a couple of guys he had met at a gas station in town. In doing so, he broke one of the cardinal rules of the industry: never do business with strangers. According to the Wanted poster that was put up around town after the murder, the men were African Americans from the Bay Area. They had followed Akselsen out on the Shelter Cove–Briceland Road in a forest green Camaro. Akselsen brought them to the privacy of the Whitethorn Junction swimming hole. It was the same place he had cooled off with Emma and his friends on so many hot summer afternoons.

As fate would have it in such a small community, a friend stumbled upon Sean Akselsen's body on her way to go swimming. He was curled up on his side on the path. He wasn't wearing a shirt, and his boxers poked out over the top of his jeans. There was a pool of blood around his head from where he had been shot.

Sean Akselsen was five months shy of his twentieth birthday.

News of his death rocked the community, but he wasn't the only person killed in marijuana business–related violence that summer. On August 11, just two weeks before Akselsen's murder, two men were reported missing. One was thirty-six-year-old Chris Giauque, a well-known pot grower and marijuana activist who used to drive around the Humboldt Hills with a "Weed Not Greed" bumper sticker on the back of his truck. Giauque was once arrested after trying to conduct a marijuana giveaway on the steps of the Humboldt County Courthouse in Eureka. On August 13, Chris Giauque's blue Toyota pickup was found abandoned along the Avenue of the Giants after he had gone on what was rumored to be a $100,000 pot deal. He is presumed dead, though his body has never been found.

Rex Shinn was also reported missing that August day. Shinn had reportedly gone to get paid for work he had done on a pot farm in the hills. Years later, people involved in Shinn's killing would lead authorities to his remains. He had been shot twice in the head and once in the neck. Marijuana-related crime was one of the top stories in Humboldt's *North Coast Journal* that year, and then-sheriff Gary Philp pointed out, "It seems to be in most cases that the violence involves deals or transactions with people from out of the area, and it appears that the clientele are people that they ought not to be dealing with."

After Sean Akselsen's murder, a memorial sprang up next to the roadside at Whitethorn Junction, not far from where he was killed. Candles, flowers, a Buddha, photographs, and other mementos of a well-loved person taken too soon were left there. Emma drove out to the memorial with her older brother and sister not long after they heard the news. She brought pictures of Sean. It was intense and heartbreaking to see everyone grieving. Emma looked around and saw people drinking bottles of Crown Royal and driving away.

The memorial for Sean Akselsen was held at Beginnings in Briceland, which was built by the Back-to-the-Land community in the late 1970s and was a cornerstone of the counterculture. The main building at Beginnings was an eight-sided structure known as the Octagon. It was the site of joyous celebrations in the community, like birthday parties, weddings, and fund-raisers, as well as sorrowful ones, like funerals. On the day of Sean Akselsen's memorial, around four hundred people gathered in the field in front of the Octagon and joined hands in an enormous circle of grief.

A microphone was passed around, and people shared memories. Emma wanted Omar to speak, but she could see that he wasn't ready yet. She also wanted to hold it together and not cry publicly. She didn't feel ready to express her grief. Then a teacher from the elementary school that Emma and Omar and Sean had all attended spoke.

When she took the microphone, she shared a memory of walking into class to teach one fall morning and first laying eyes on two beautiful little boys named Sean and Omar. The rest of the story was lost in Emma's mind, because all it took was that image of the two boys with their whole lives and futures ahead of them for the floodgates to open and the tears to come pouring out. All those memories of Sean came rushing back to Emma.

He had been like a family member to her, and now he was gone.

Not long after Sean's death, another friend of Omar's, a boy named Neil, was electrocuted while trying to lift a downed wire off the road. Then Emma's ex-boyfriend Kaleb Garza was killed. Garza had been driving his motorcycle up a friend's driveway. His brother Nate happened to be coming down that same road in a truck. One of the boys didn't have headlights and was using a giant flashlight to light his way. The truck and the motorcycle collided, and as is often the case, the motorcycle lost. The photo of Kaleb that ran in the paper with the news of his death was taken at his senior prom. He looked happy and dapper in his suit with a burgundy cummerbund; cropped out of the photos was a freshman with auburn ringlets and a pale green dress.

The sad-ass stories kept coming. Emma's good friend's brother Kioma Wise was killed in a four-wheeler accident, and mystery swirled around his death. The pain from the loss and the unanswered questions around the death caused Emma's friend to move away. Then a girl at school hanged herself in her bedroom. Craig Eichen died in a car accident. It began to feel to Emma that if you were a young person and went out to party and drove on dirt roads, there was a good chance you were going to get killed. Emma figured it was what every person who lived in a rural community experienced, that growing up anywhere was like growing up in Southern Humboldt. As a child, she just assumed that her surroundings were normal. A few years later, she would prove herself wrong.

CHAPTER SEVEN

Bob

Early one Sunday morning, Bob Hamilton sat at the secretary's desk in the sheriff's substation in Garberville and surfed the Net. Outside, the rain fell heavily and steadily, as it had for days, giving new meaning to the term *rain forest*. Bob hated the substation, a squat cinderblock building located next to the fire department on Locust Street. He found it shabby and embarrassing. He also suspected that it contained asbestos and lead paint, which is one of the many reasons he preferred to be out on patrol. Bob's office was his car, but sometimes he needed to swing by the substation to fill out paperwork or, in this case, check the news online.

After a quick glance at the headlines, he headed for a white sedan parked out front. He began his rounds while most of the town was still asleep. Normally, he rolled in an Expedition, but it was being upgraded to a new model—much to his chagrin, during the rainy season, when the SUV's four-wheel drive was particularly useful on the dirt roads that turned to mud. After he swung a left onto Main Street, Bob pulled over to send a quick text to his wife, who was visiting their daughter, who was in her junior year at the University of California at Davis.

"Have a good day, dear," he wrote.

Main Street in Garberville, otherwise known as Redwood Drive, is about four blocks long. Considering its reputation as the epicenter of America's marijuana industry, it is an underwhelming place. It has no stoplight, and only one stop sign. The street is lined with three gas stations, a handful of motels, a movie theater, a grocery store called Ray's Food Place, and an array of small businesses, none of which is a national chain—except for the Radio Shack on Maple Lane, which may well be the only electronics store in America with a fabric store attached. Among Garberville's other institutions are a barbershop that sells guns, a coffee shop called Flavors, and the Eel River Café, whose neon sign, featuring a man in chef's whites flipping a pancake, is as much a symbol of the town as the pot leaf sign at the Hemp Connection across the street.

The way Bob saw it, everything in town revolved around the dope industry. Businesses catered either to the sale and production of marijuana directly—like Dazey's Supply, a commercial grow store that sold millions of dollars' worth of soil every year—or to the women who dated wealthy growers, which was the reason there was a day spa on Main Street. Among its services, Humboldt Hunnies offered Brazilian waxes and organic skin care products to a clientele that included what Bob liked to call "potstitutes," attractive young women whose social uniform consisted of skinny jeans, long hair, and fake breasts. Bob hadn't coined the term *potstitute*—it was local slang—but using it made him cackle with glee.

At the top of the street near the Umpqua Bank, Bob waved to an older man in an orange sweatshirt.

"Hi!" Bob yelled out his window.

Robert Firestone was in his eighties and had dementia. He was known to wander. Bob tried to keep tabs on him so that when Firestone's family called, he could tell them where he'd last seen the old man. The following month, Robert Firestone would wander off for good, and his face would become a familiar one as he peered out from the Missing Person posters plastered all over town. A two-day search of the area was conducted by boat and helicopter, but Robert Firestone was never seen again. On this day, however, he raised his arm and waved.

Next, Bob began to drive around the town's motels, or "drug fronts," as he called them. There were four he normally patrolled, including his favorite, Johnston's Quality Motel, which seemed most popular with the meth freaks.

Johnston's Quality Motel was located behind the Getti Up drive-through coffee shack, where girls in low-cut tops served drinks to go. The motel was painted a faded cotton candy pink, and even in the light of day it exuded an ominous vibe, like some kind of backwoods Bates Motel. As Bob pulled past the entrance at a crawl, he greeted the motel manager, a small South Asian man who was standing outside.

"Namaste!" Bob chirped.

His cruiser crawled along the front of the train-car-shaped building, past doors to rooms where he had made too many arrests to count—for dope, heroin, and meth. Bob shook his head and repeated the name of the hotel over and over again, placing special emphasis on the ill-fitting adjective.

"Johnston's Quality Motel. Johnston's Q-u-a-l-i-t-y Motel."

From the motel parking lot, Bob spied a woman he knew. She was in front of the Shell gas station across the street, scratching a lottery ticket next to the entrance to the station's mini-mart. Like a child who didn't want to be seen, she turned when Bob pulled up alongside her, facing the wall as if she were hiding.

"Where's your paint gun, Barbara?" Bob asked.

"You took it away from me," she snapped. "Leave me alone."

Barbara was missing most of her teeth, and her face was covered in the kind of scabs that indicate heavy methamphetamine use. A couple of miles away, a minivan was covered with splotches of paint. It belonged to Barbara's daughter. Bob had taken away Barbara's paint gun after she shot up her daughter's van.

"What a freak," Bob said as he pulled away and headed past the limestone bluffs and the Eel River and toward Redway.

The area Bob covered was around 1,200 square miles and, as he saw, it, severely underserved. Sometimes he'd be the only person on call in all of Southern Humboldt. He had no idea how many people lived there; no one seemed to. There were only 135,000 people in the entire county, and most of them lived up north, around the cities of Eureka and Arcata. Some estimated that the population of Southern Humboldt was around 15,000 to 20,000, but there was no good official number, given that many people who lived there weren't the type who would respond to a census.

Bob kept track by the communities he patrolled. He carried a slip of weathered yellow paper tucked in his car visor on which he'd composed a list of the various towns and hamlets; some were official settlements, some were not. There were twenty-nine in all: Pepperwood, Redcrest, Holmes Flat, Weott, Myers Flat, Miranda, Phillipsville, Garberville, Redway, Briceland, Whitethorn, Ettersburg, Honeydew, Petrolia, Alderpoint, Harris, New Harris, Shelter Cove, Benbow, Blocksburg, French Camp, Capetown, Bear River, McCann, Eel Rock, Fort Seward, Shively, Ocean House, and Island Mountain, a remote place known to growers as the geographic center of the Emerald Triangle.

On Sunset Avenue in Redway, Bob pulled his car over in front of a house surrounded by a high fence. Many of the houses in Redway had exceedingly tall, fortress-like fences. Bob had been to this house before, and knew that, come fall, pot plants ten feet tall would poke above the top of the fence. The people who lived in the house sold their pot to a collective, which would distribute or sell it to its members on a nonprofit basis, according to state law. Last year, Bob knocked on the door and informed the people living there that they needed to affix to their gate their 215, the doctor's recommendation that gave them the legal right to grow pot. He needed to be able to read it with his binoculars.

In the busy season, from late summer and into the fall, Bob did a lot of inspections to make sure people had their 215s and that the amount they were growing was in accordance with the law. His goal was to try to keep people in compliance and from getting too greedy.

Bob swung his car around in front of Dazey's Motorsports, a shop that sells four-wheelers and Rhinos, like Crockett used, which are particularly handy for reaching remote pot patches in the hills. He thought again about how the war on marijuana was over. This whole 215 thing was a joke. It was like a license to be a criminal. The government needed to get some *cojones* and either make pot legal, or make it entirely illegal. He learned a long time ago that nothing was going to stop it. It was better to just get real about it. If Bob knew anything, it was how to be real.

———

Bob Hamilton was born in Los Angeles County in 1961. When he was around seven, his parents moved the family to Ferndale, a central Humboldt town of picturesque Victorians and conservative leanings. It was the kind of place in the early 1970s where a "We Drink Hippie Blood" sign hung in the town's Hotel Ivanhoe bar. Bob was the eldest of four. His father was a navy man who ran his family with a firm hand. In 1972, when Bob was ten, his father came home drunk, pointed a loaded .22 rifle at Bob's mother, and pulled the trigger. Bob's father then walked to the local bar and ordered himself a drink before he told the bartender to call the sheriff because he had just killed his wife.

Ten-year-old Bob came out of his bedroom that night and discovered his mother covered in blood. Miraculously, she survived the shooting, though she was left blind in one eye and lost her sense of smell. Bob never saw his father again, but heard that the navy sent him to Vietnam, and that he survived the war and later settled in Texas. His mother, meanwhile, moved the children north to Eureka.

Bob attended junior high in Eureka and worked odd jobs after school to help support his family. In his spare time he loved to wander in Sequoia Park, a patch of ancient forest located in the middle of a residential neighborhood. The grove was a testament to what Eureka looked like before redwoods were chopped down as the city expanded. Bob could spend all day there; it was his own Lost World.

Inside the park it was quiet and cool, and there were dirt paths to race down that were lined with giant sword ferns. Slimy yellow banana slugs inched along in the shade. Bob liked to climb around on the huge stumps of fallen trees. He loved their massiveness, and their beauty and tranquility. To walk among them felt like swimming among blue whales. Enveloped by the trees and the earthy smell of redwood needles and forest floor, Bob felt safe and at peace. It was in Sequoia Park where his lifelong love of redwoods was born.

Around this same time, Bob's lifelong "sensitivity" to marijuana began. He was fourteen the first and only time he smoked pot. He was hanging out after school with his best friend and his best friend's parents. The family was all smoking weed out of a hookah pipe in the living room. Bob's friend suggested Bob give it a try. He shook his head. Then the mother started in; she said if Bob tried it just once, they'd leave him alone. So he pressed his lips against the mouthpiece and drew in a lungful of smoke. Then he had a most unusual, almost allergic reaction: he began to projectile-vomit all over the living room. After that, everyone in school knew not to give Bob any pot.

Bob's mother died in a horrific fire later that same year, and he was separated from his siblings and sent to live with relatives in Southern California. Bob credits the counseling he received after his mother's death with saving him. He was lost and broken, but he eventually learned that his past did not have to define him, and he wasn't destined for perpetual tragedy. His fundamentally upbeat nature no doubt helped as well. Bob joined the air force after graduation, married his high school sweetheart, and they had a daughter. He then served thirteen years as a cop in the Central Valley city of Fresno. Every year, he would find a way back to his beloved Humboldt to visit. The beauty of the place would call him home. After retiring from the Fresno Police Department in 2000, Bob made good on his dream and brought his family back to Humboldt for good. Or so he thought.

Now he couldn't wait to leave. It was spoiled for him. Behind every beautiful vista, Bob now saw dope, and meth, and what he called the "junkyard lifestyle" of those living on the edge. When he retired, he planned on packing up and leaving Humboldt County the very next day.

———

Continuing on his way to Shelter Cove, just before the Honeydew-Ettersburg Junction, Bob swung his cruiser to the shoulder and pulled around so he was facing the road. He shut off his engine and sat back in his seat. It was time to play the little game he called Scare the Shit out of the Dope Growers.

The idea was that if the drivers and passengers in the passing cars looked over at Bob, they were up to something and would most likely pass along word to their friends that a deputy was parked near the junction and headed to Shelter Cove. If no one bothered to glance over at Bob as they drove by, he figured they were law-abiding citizens.

A large blue truck rumbled past. The young male driver turned and checked out the sheriff's vehicle.

There it was, Bob figured. The "phone tree" will have started, which was the point of the game, really, to get the dope growers buzzing and worried even though he wasn't actually on the hunt.

The first time Bob drove this road in an official vehicle, four years earlier, a few cars were waiting for him when he reached Shelter Cove. The drivers waved him down. They had heard Bob was on his way and wanted to report some recent robberies, including a stolen lawn mower and four-wheeler. Bob asked how they knew he was coming.

One of the guys told him that a buddy in San Francisco had called him.

"How did your buddy in San Francisco know I was coming?" Bob asked.

Somebody had called *him*, was the reply.

The same thing would happen when Bob drove up to any of the far-flung communities he patrolled. It was outlaw mentality to spread the word when law enforcement was in the area. "Visitors are on the hill" was one common telephone code to announce their presence. The system worked so well that an entire hillside could be alerted within fifteen minutes of the first sighting of a federal convoy or a sheriff's SUV. Back at the station, Kenny Swithenbank called it the "coconut telegraph," after the Jimmy Buffett song. Whenever they were headed out into the hills to a place like Alderpoint, looking to arrest someone on a warrant, the deputies would take the back way, through Fort Seward or Eel Rock, to avoid arriving in a ghost town.

A white Toyota roared past. Then came a blue Ford F-150 with two pit bulls in the back. Some of the drivers turned their heads to look at Bob; others just whizzed by.

After a few minutes, Bob started his car back up and continued on his journey to the coast. He passed by the roadside memorial for Sean Akselsen. Seven years after his murder, it was still well tended with fake flowers and mementos spilling out from a mosaic altar. The falling rain splattered noisily on Bob's windshield as he drove by Whitethorn Construction, a lumber and building supply company run by a tall octogenarian with a bushy beard named Bob McKee. In the 1960s and '70s, McKee became famous in the area for subdividing old ranches and selling parcels to the new settlers. Many members of the counterculture considered him the father of their community.

"I was looking to sell the land to people who really wanted it," McKee explained to local journalist Mary Siler Anderson in her book *Whatever Happened to the Hippies?* McKee didn't care if someone had driven the two hundred miles from San Francisco on a Vespa or if they had arrived in a converted potato chip truck. If they loved the place and wanted to live there, he was willing to sell them land.

As for the cash crop that so many people eventually planted on land he sold them, at first, McKee said he had no idea marijuana could even grow in Humboldt; he thought it came from India or some other exotic place. He didn't seem to care much about it as a moral issue, but he had the foresight to worry when pot became valuable.

It was the start of what McKee called a "false economy."

"I guess my concern was what people were going to do when it was gone," he said, decades before community members would gather at the Mateel to discuss that very issue. "I knew the money was going to go away. Either it was going to get wiped out or it was going to be legalized, but one way or the other it was going away."

For Bob Hamilton, it couldn't go away soon enough.

Past Whitethorn Construction, the trees were barely visible through the mist as Bob entered the King Range National Conservation Area. At the top of the peak, his radio crackled. He eased the cruiser over to the side of the road and called in to dispatch.

Someone had just reported that a man armed with two AR-15 assault rifles was going to be doing a series of armed robberies of indoor marijuana grows in the town of Fortuna. Bob was instructed to be on the lookout for the guy's vehicle.

"This should be interesting," Bob said to dispatch. Then he plunged down the steep, windy road that led to Shelter Cove.

The Cove, as it is known to locals, is situated on the Lost Coast, a place that frontier writer Bret Harte called "America's uttermost west." It earned its name back in the 1930s, when engineers building the Pacific Coast Highway were forced to turn inland and bypass the area because of its steep, rugged terrain. That decision helped create the longest undeveloped stretch of coastline in California. It is now a popular three-day hike for backpackers, and a place where the mountains of the King Range drop dramatically into the ocean. At Cape Mendocino the land juts out at the state's westernmost point. Offshore, three fault lines, including the infamous San Andreas, meet and rub shoulders.

Shelter Cove, the only town on the Lost Coast, was established as a resort in 1964. Developers envisioned four thousand homes overlooking the sea there. Lots were sold, sight unseen, but many were so steep that it was impossible to build on them, and Shelter Cove became a land swindle. Today the Cove is a small village of some seven hundred residents who must drive an hour of windy road to cover the twenty miles to the nearest grocery store. Bob estimated that about half of these residents were pot growers who had turned their homes into indoor gardens.

On this wet and rainy Sunday, he drove past houses with uninspiring architecture and tiny blue street signs warning that the area was in a tsunami zone. Bob cruised by the golf course, and the Cape Mendocino Tea House, and pulled around Wedding Point, where surfers check the waves with binoculars and paragliders set sail. He eased to a stop in front of a sporty blue Subaru that was parked next to a row of houses. The car's owner had done seven years in federal prison for marijuana cultivation. He was also Bob's friend.

The two men rode motorcycles together. Like many Southern Humboldt men, Bob's friend was a member of a local volunteer fire department. Bob's theory was that many growers became members of local fire departments out of guilt over how they earn their money. Another, more dire reason was that there was nobody else to provide emergency services in the hills of Humboldt, where it could take an ambulance well over an hour to reach the scene of an accident. Neighbors literally had to save each other's lives.

It was an uneventful morning at the Cove, and after Bob finished driving through town, he headed up the mountain and back toward Redway. On his way, he pulled into the Shelter Cove General Store to refuel. The general store was the kind of place where the wooden floors creaked underfoot and gas was sold at inflated prices, even by Humboldt standards. You could buy a bottle of soda and a bag of chips there, or, in Bob's case, Milk Duds and a V-8.

On his way back from the bathroom, something caught Bob's eye that made him bound through the store's double doors in a fit of laughter.

"What's with that sign 'Robert's in Jail'?" he asked the clerk behind the register, a woman whose husband he had once arrested for growing pot.

"I had to think for a minute who Robert was," Bob continued before she could answer. "It's Buddha. I forget that's his name."

"Yeah, that's Buddha," the woman said quietly.

Robert Juan, more commonly known in the community as Buddha, was the man Emma and her stepbrother Mike had once worked for. In 2003, Buddha met an old logger with a thousand acres of land for sale. Buddha then formed the Lost Paradise Land Corp., and began offering people a chance to buy into the corporation with a hefty down payment. They could then live on the land and make small monthly payments. Around forty people purchased a stake in the place. Many, if not all, did what they do in Humboldt, and grew pot there. They called the settlement Buddhaville, after its founder.

The Feds called it a criminal conspiracy.

On June 24, 2008, an army of 450 federal and law enforcement agents raided Buddhaville. People would remember that each agent seemed to have his own unmarked SUV or sedan, for the convoy of vehicles that passed along the Briceland–Shelter Cove Road on the way to the bust seemed endless. Authorities hauled off ten thousand marijuana plants, $160,000 in cash, and thirty guns. Buddha was eventually given a five-year sentence. All those who invested in the land lost their money. During the backlash following the bust, someone burnt down Buddha's house.

"Robert's in Jail," the piece of binder paper tacked to the bulletin board in front of the store read. "For four plus years."

In looping, feminine cursive, the sign instructed anyone who wanted to write Buddha to put their name on a list, and Buddha would send a note initiating correspondence. It was signed by a woman named Holly, with that morning's date.

Bob was still chuckling as he started up the cruiser and pointed it back up the mountain. Twenty miles or so down the road, just past the turnout to Seeley Creek, a muddy track marked by a row of mailboxes, Bob saw something that he had never noticed before, something that made him gasp, and temporarily forget about marijuana and all his other frustrations.

He flipped the cruiser around and doubled back. About a hundred feet away, on the other side of the creek, a clear stream of rainwater cascaded down a stone cliff. Trees growing at the top of the fall looked as though they might tumble off. The scene was so lush and green it looked like it belonged on a postcard from Kauai. Bob sat there in silence and took in the beauty of the place, and just for a moment he was reminded why he'd come home.

CHAPTER EIGHT

Crockett

The day of the first rain, Crockett Randall was sitting on a couch next to his truck in a field filled with thousands of revelers when he noticed the storm clouds moving dark and heavy across the mid-September sky. It was six weeks before the vote, and the second day of Earthdance, a three-day music festival headlined by Michael Franti at the Black Oak Ranch in Laytonville. The northern Mendocino County town was another Emerald Triangle institution and a throwback to the 1960s. It was home to a store dedicated entirely to tie-dye and to Wavy Gravy's Hog Farm, which claimed to be the longest-running hippie commune in America.

Crockett had taken a couple of days off to attend the festival. Frankie wasn't too happy about it, but Crockett needed a break from playing guard dog at the cabin, and he intended to make the two-hour return trip every day to check on the plants. So far, he had avoided getting busted or robbed. But now, as the raindrops began to fall, at first in a sprinkle, then in a full downpour, there was Mother Nature to contend with, and it was about to get ugly.

Crockett left Earthdance early the next morning and drove back to the garden at his usual breakneck speed. He immediately began his rounds. Even though the plants were supposedly protected from the elements by the white plastic sheeting that enveloped the greenhouses, in reality, the stuff was flimsy. Crockett called it toilet paper. It was so permeable that when he shook the branches of the plants after that first rain, water leapt off in heavy droplets. He called Frankie immediately to report what he was seeing.

"It's not good, man," he said.

As harvest approached, Crockett had been hypervigilant about mold. It could destroy an entire crop. He checked for it daily. The signs were subtle, barely discernable to the untrained eye. Sometimes, something as simple as a leaf that was starting to curl on a stacked flower cluster was enough to indicate that, inside, thousands of dollars' worth of bud was turning to rotten mush.

Crockett liked to joke that plants were ready to harvest when the money guy was in town, but in reality, he'd examine the buds with a magnifying glass, like the most exacting of growers, to determine if the trichomes—the microscopic, crystalline resin droplets on the flower's surface—had turned a milky white and if the resinous, hairlike parts called pistils had turned red and brown. When this happened, the plants were ready to be cut. But sometimes, you had to speed up the process. When, two days after the rains began, the sun broke through the clouds and cast its warm rays once again on the hills of Humboldt, Crockett and Zavie scrambled to begin harvest. Otherwise, the heat, combined with the dampness from the recent rain, would turn all the thick, heavy flower clusters into perfect petri dishes for mold.

Normally, a marijuana harvest follows a straightforward, relatively simple, if not strenuous process. Whether the plants are grown indoors or out, when the trichomes and resin glands indicate they are ready, the branches bearing the heavy flower clusters, or "colas," are lopped off and hung upside down to dry. Waterleaves, those trademark five-fingered leaves, grow and fan out from the colas, giving them a fuzzy look. Some growers prefer to pull these larger outer leaves off before the drying process begins; others leave them for trimmers to sift through later.

Over the course of a few days, as the hanging buds dry in barns, sheds, and backrooms, they shrink to about 50 percent of their original size. The dried buds are then placed in paper bags, and as with tobacco, a curing process begins. When the buds reach the right consistency—which varies according to each grower but is usually some level of crispy on the outside and slightly moist on the inside—they are ready to be processed, or trimmed.

Many things can and do go wrong along the way during harvest, and things took a wrong turn for Crockett and his crew almost immediately. On the day that the sun broke through the clouds after the first rain, Crockett and Zavie started cutting down the plants because mold had started popping like a virus they couldn't control. They began by chopping off all the top branches on the plants, and bringing in the largest, most valuable colas. By the time they were ready for a second round, though, the mold had spread fast.

Then the bottleneck began.

In preparation for harvest, Frankie had helped Crockett construct a temporary drying shed next to the cabin. They filled it with white clothes hangers from which they planned to hang the pot. The cabin itself was also turned into a drying room. The bed where Crockett slept and stored his gun was pushed against the wall to make room for the weed, and he took to sleeping in the loft. Wire was strung back and forth across the cabin ceiling like an Italian clothesline, and they hung pot branches from it. But there still wasn't enough room. The mold was coming so quickly they had to cut all the plants and bring them in at once. Even with the extra drying shed, there just didn't seem to be enough room.

At one point, they filled the beds of both Crockett's and Frankie's trucks with hundreds of thousands of dollars' worth of plants, which they then dumped on the cabin floor. Green, fragrant branches covered the entire room. Crockett was literally up to his shins in it. They were working fifteen-hour days, and he was exhausted. There was no escape. Even when Crockett slept, he was surrounded by weed. Then, some of the people Frankie had hired to help with the harvest hung the colas together too tightly in the shed, and mold began to spread there, too. Crockett was pissed.

"Nobody's allowed to pack this weed but me," he told Frankie.

Despite Crockett's best efforts, the cabin floor was soon littered with paper grocery bags full of gray, hairy, rotten buds that looked like something that could grow inside a cottage cheese container forgotten in the back of the fridge. The year 2010 would go down as one of epic mold in Humboldt County. Maybe it was nature's revenge for the greed and panic that had prompted so many people to plant more than they ever had before, because of the threat of legalization. Whatever the reason, when all was said and done, Crockett, Frankie, and Zavie lost around a quarter of their crop—the equivalent of about $250,000 in cash.

Just as the Napa Valley, a few hours south, fills with the smell of fermenting grapes during harvest season, the skunky forbidden odor of marijuana hangs over the hills of Humboldt every fall. But whereas in Napa, tourists can line up to see the grapes brought into the crush pad to begin their journey to the bottle, in Humboldt, the marijuana harvest goes on behind high fences and locked gates, and up dusty roads.

The harvest of America's favorite illegal drug is a private affair.

In Crockett's cabin, the trimmers sat in a circle around the table and hunched over trays that contained their scissors, cleaning solution, and crispy little piles of marijuana buds. It was hot, so the door was left open and fans whirled day and night to cool off the workers and help dry the buds that hung in clumps from the wires above like mutant mistletoe. The trimmers were women for the most part, in keeping with the industry practice. A typical trim scene usually consists of a group of women, with the occasional man thrown in, listening to music, sharing stories, and clipping marijuana. There was something almost traditional about it, like a quilting circle of older times. Throughout Humboldt, grandmothers, students, service industry workers, and teenagers such as Emma Worldpeace supplemented their income with trim work every year or did it full time. These particular women were friends of Frankie and his girlfriend from the Bay Area, and people whom the couple had met while traveling in Costa Rica.

As far as under-the-table manual labor was concerned, trimming was a lucrative gig. Marijuana trimmers were usually paid for the amount of product they cleaned. The going rate for trimmers in the fall of 2010 was $200 a pound. Cash. Which meant that relatively fast trimmers, who averaged a pound a day, could earn at least $25 an hour. Tax-free, of course. Seasoned pros could trim double or sometimes even triple that. It all depended on the weight and quality of the pot. Given the private, homebound nature of the business, many trimmers were also housed and fed by their employers. Frankie's trimmers stayed on couches at his place near Garberville, on air mattresses on the floor, and in the RV out front. One slept outside in a tent. There was a festive, slumber-party feel to it all, at least for the first few days, until the novelty wore off and the sheer drudgery of the work set in.

To clean, trim, clip, manicure, or process pot for sale, a trimmer begins by cutting off any protruding leaves with sewing scissors. Then she trims around the dried flower bud to make it look like a tidy round hedge. Itchy green flakes fly off in the process and stick to clothing, become lodged in hair, and slip down bras. Most trimmers wear aprons. Some wear gloves to prevent their fingers from becoming coated in sticky brown residue. When the bud is uniform and neat, the trimmer drops it in a container next to her, cleans off her scissors if they have become unwieldy due to the resin, and then starts all over again. And again. And again.

It is painfully tedious work, but because of the relatively high wages, there is never a shortage of people willing to do it. Every fall, the streets and businesses of Humboldt see an influx of new faces. Along with the transients who drive Bob crazy, many of these faces belong to people who already have jobs lined up and places to stay. Because of the fear of rip-offs and the general illegality of the business, most Humboldt growers don't hire trimmers off the street. Some import their labor. Trimmers come from all over: ski bums from Utah, carpenters from Vermont, teachers from Hawaii, people met while traveling in Costa Rica. Like the growers who employ them, they are predominately white.

In a way, they are California's last white migrant farm workers.

Clear plastic turkey-roasting bags are the industry standard for packaging marijuana. They are cheap and they nicely hold a pound. When the turkey bags full of freshly trimmed pot that escaped the mold began to pile up, Crockett began moving them south, out of the county. The idea was to sell as much as possible as quickly as possible, before the glut began and prices dropped, like they did every year after harvest. That wasn't taking into account whatever was going to happen with the vote in November. A connection in Sonoma County was buying at $3,400 a pound, which was high for marijuana grown outdoors in a greenhouse. Crockett figured the guy would probably sell it as indoor pot on the black market. He had no idea where it would end up, but guessed it would be some state back east, where pot was still illegal. A lot of what Crockett used to sell would go to Colorado, but then voters there approved a medical marijuana law of their own, and that place, as he put it, blew up.

Crockett packed fifteen to twenty pounds of pot in a waterproof bag that the man who sold it to him said was popularized by Navy SEALs. It wasn't the water he worried about so much as the smell. The waterproof bag wouldn't stand up to a drug-detection dog, but it should fool a cop. A few weeks earlier, Crockett had been pulled over again for speeding, near Myers Flat. He was in full harvest mode, and his clothes reeked of pot.

"Where is it?" the highway patrol officer demanded after Crockett rolled down his window and hit him with the smell.

The officer handcuffed Crockett and put him in the backseat of his car while he searched the vehicle. Fortunately, Crockett didn't have anything on him, and he eventually drove away a free man.

Crockett deposited the bag in his trunk and started up his car. His first stop would be the car wash in Redway, where he would blast the layer of fine, pale dirt off his Mitsubishi with a high-powered hose. He had heard that police looked for dirty cars to pull over on the gauntlet south, the dust a telltale sign of a journey up unpaved roads to places where pot plants grow. The medical marijuana card in Crockett's pocket wouldn't cover what he was about to do. The transportation of marijuana was a gray area in the state's medical marijuana law, and was basically illegal. Crockett slammed his trunk shut, cranked up his stereo, and headed south on the Redwood Highway, for once driving the speed limit.

———

Around the same time that Crockett began hauling the first of the year's harvest south, an unusual meeting was being held on Marina Way in Eureka. The Medical Cannabis Ordinance Workshop was cohosted by a newly founded group called the Humboldt Growers Association and by county supervisor Bonnie Neely. The purpose of the workshop was to discuss how Humboldt County might finally begin to regulate its infamous clandestine industry. Panelists included the Humboldt district attorney; two members of the board of supervisors; Joey Burger, the president of the Growers Association; and a lobbyist the association had hired who looked eerily like Clark Kent.

During part of the meeting, Bob Hamilton's boss, Sheriff Gary Philp, sat in the audience.

The Humboldt County D.A., Paul Gallegos, was the only prosecutor in the entire state to come out publicly in favor of Prop 19. The way Gallegos saw it, the federal government was on the right side of history with abolishing slavery, and on the wrong side when it came to marijuana. If Prop 19 passed the following month, the law would leave it up to cities and counties to tax and regulate the marijuana industry how they saw fit. At the meeting, Gallegos welcomed the beginning of what he saw as a long-overdue discussion on how that regulation should look.

"We're a decade late," he said that day. "We spent a long time addressing this as an illegitimate industry."

The Bay Area city of Oakland was ahead of the curve and had recently approved plans to permit large-scale marijuana-growing operations within city limits. In Humboldt, the answer wasn't "pot factories," as people were calling the Oakland model, but pot farms. At the meeting, the Humboldt Growers Association passed out copies of its proposed ordinance, which would license and tax outdoor grows, from $20,000 for a quarter acre to $80,000 for an acre.

"Cannabis farmers want to pay taxes," said Joey Burger, the association's president, a serious-looking man in his late twenties with a trim beard and short brown hair. Burger repeated the refrain that, with legalization, Humboldt could become "the new Napa of Cannabis."

In calling it cannabis, Burger used the term that dispensary owners and others in the business had begun employing in the media in an effort to be taken more seriously. As Max Del Real, the lobbyist, explained, "Pot is the drug, cannabis is the commodity."

That afternoon, there was talk of marijuana certification, testing, and insurance. The commercialization and legalization of the industry was a whole new world, and similar to the "What's After Pot?" meeting held earlier in the year, everyone in the room knew how important it was for the people in Humboldt County to secure a place in that world to avoid a total collapse of their economy. As Burger explained a few weeks before the meeting, "I don't want to see tumbleweeds blowing through my town."

CHAPTER NINE

Mare

In the decades between the discovery of sinsemilla and the looming legalization vote that threatened to turn Garberville and Redway into ghost towns, with tumbleweed blowing through, time passed for Mare Abidon in a cyclical fashion. Throughout the 1980s, she supplemented her work as an art teacher and her newfound forest activism by growing a small amount of marijuana. Many people grew on public land in those days—or on private land that didn't belong to them. The latter was called guerrilla growing, and it reduced a grower's chance of getting caught if his patch were raided. Plants grown on public property are nearly impossible to trace. Like many people in her community then, Mare and her two partners grew in the King Range National Conservation Area, a 68,000-acre mountainous wilderness area located near her cabin.

The years passed, marked by quiet winters long with rain, when chanterelle mushrooms the size of dinner plates would grow wild on the forest floor. In the spring, bright orange poppies and purple lupine would appear along the roadside, marijuana seeds would sprout and be sown, and Mare would put on an Easter Bunny suit and hop down to the meadow to entertain the children during the annual community egg hunt. Hot, dry summers were followed by the busy harvest season. Mare's life was interspersed by occasional love affairs, and actions to save the last of the old-growth redwoods from being clear-cut.

But there were moments during this blur of time that Mare recognized as turning points. Sometimes they were dramatic, like the arrival of the helicopters that buzzed low over the hills to take out plant after plant, grower after grower. Other times, they were gradual, like the awareness that some of her friends had started to make a lot of money off pot, not just to sustain a counterculture lifestyle, but also to achieve something that looked more like the American Dream they had supposedly left behind. Some bought nicer cars, built bigger houses, and began to take long vacations to faraway places. Then there was the danger element that came creeping in, and with it, outsiders who were willing to hurt people. The most horrific example was what happened to Kathy Davis.

Mare first met Kathy Davis in 1970, during that first summer in Humboldt when she helped her cousin build a house. Davis was a social worker who had come from Berkeley in 1968 with her husband and young daughter. She was a pillar in her community. She sat on the county grand jury, and on the board of the local credit union. She cofounded the Garberville Hospice to provide care for the dying, and was the kind of person who would watch your baby for you while you were sick. She raised chickens and planted iris bulbs. Like so many in her community, Kathy Davis also grew pot.

Mare loved Kathy. She thought she was a firecracker. The last time Mare saw her, Davis told her how much she was looking forward to growing older. But she never got that chance. In September of 1982, Davis was beaten and strangled to death in her drying room by two men who had come to rob her. She was thirty-eight years old. Two weeks later, her cremated remains were scattered around the apricot tree in her front yard. At her memorial a group of longhaired men and women dressed in faded jeans and sundresses held hands around a small pond, linked in grief and shattered ideals. Mare stood among them. Everyone sang "Amazing Grace," and Mare thought to herself, My God, everything is changing.

Even more change was to come, like years later, when the United States government invaded.

On the morning of July 29, 1990, the seventeen-year-old daughter of one of Mare's neighbors went for a walk near her home by the coast. As Blossom Edwards strolled through the woods, she came upon five or six men lying on the forest floor. They had camouflage smeared on their faces and automatic weapons that were pointed right at her.

"Hey, who are you?" Blossom asked. "What is going on?"

The men wouldn't respond. As soon as Blossom returned home, word about her encounter with the men with guns traveled through the community quickly, by CB radio and by phone. It was the first that many people in Southern Humboldt heard about "Operation Green Sweep."

The men, it turned out, were part of a group of some two hundred army soldiers, National Guardsmen, and federal agents who had been sent to Humboldt by President George H. W. Bush to destroy illicit gardens and remove the irrigation systems, water tanks, and other infrastructure used to grow them in the King Range National Conservation Area, the place where Mare used to grow. The soldiers were members of the Seventh Infantry Division who had recently helped depose Manuel Noriega during the Panama invasion.

The army's arrival in Southern Humboldt marked the first time in U.S. history that active-duty troops were used to enforce domestic laws in a nonemergency situation.

The size of the domestic marijuana crop had apparently become an embarrassment for the first Bush administration. At an antidrug summit in Cartagena, Colombia, earlier that year, during a conversation about that country's coca crop, the Colombian president had asked Bush about the marijuana grown on the North Coast of California. Operation Green Sweep was Bush's response. As a government spokesperson told members of the media during the operation, it was undertaken to show our southern neighbors and people around the country that the Bush administration took marijuana growing seriously. His drug czar, William Bennett, identified California as the "epicenter of America's drug problem."

Mare was livid when she heard about Green Sweep. She couldn't believe that her own government had come into her community and pointed guns at her friend's daughter, and that her own army was being used against her. It was as if they had forgotten that she and her friends were Americans, too, regardless of the plants they grew. In true Southern Humboldt style, Mare and a bunch of other outraged community members headed down to the meadow called Hidden Valley, which was being used as the military staging area. There, at the edge of the sprawling wilderness area, across a dirt road from men with guns and camouflage vehicles and Black Hawk helicopters, they held a protest that was surely like nothing the authorities had ever seen before.

Word spread, and people showed up in Volvos and pickup trucks. They brought their children and their indignation, which they expressed on hand-painted signs they waved in the air:

"Plants Can't Shoot and They Can't Run, So Why Bring the Guns?" read one placard.

"Yanqui, Go Home Grown" advised another.

A few people in the crowd held up "U.S. Out of Humboldt County" bumper stickers.

Despite the outrage, because this was Humboldt, there was a carnival-like air to the protest. A little girl blew bubbles. The Garberville Marimba Band set up its enormous xylophones under a tree and made music that sounded like falling rain. There were lots of beards and tie-dye, a man in a coyote mask, and a Ronald Reagan impersonator in a pink sports coat who gave an animated speech reminding everyone how the Declaration of Independence was signed on paper made of hemp.

Across the dusty road, a group of highway patrol officers with thick moustaches and aviator shades warily observed the spectacle unfolding in front of them.

At one point, Hoy, a woman who two decades later would say of the marijuana industry, "Peaceful hippies, my ass, this is all about greed," broke into song next to a group of lawmen, while a friend filmed the encounter. Hoy wore army fatigues, and her short dreadlocks peeked out from under a flak helmet.

"They destroyed our black history," she sang at the top of her lungs, grinning and leaning in close, seemingly taunting the men until they dispersed.

The protest vigil continued throughout the two-week Green Sweep.

On August 2, about fifty members of the local and national media were given a tour of the operation. During the press conference beforehand, the national director of the Bureau of Land Management of the U.S. Department of the Interior, Delos "Cy" Jamison, explained the message of Green Sweep. "We won't tolerate unlawful drug activity on public lands," he said. "It's a crime we have to spend this much time and manpower doing it."

Jamison showed the press some of the growing materials they had pulled out of the forest, which included chicken wire, flowerpots, fish emulsion fertilizer, plastic waterlines, and a surfboard. The idea was if they removed these things, the growers wouldn't return.

"If they come back, we'll come back," he threatened. "We're serious about that, because it fits in with our national drug strategy."

Later, as journalists passed by the protest on their way to the Green Sweep encampment, they were warned the demonstrators were likely to turn riotous at any time.

The protestors never went berserk, but there was an attempt to challenge the government's presence. At one point, seven people, including Mare, decided to take a stand by crossing the official perimeter.

Mare knew she risked arrest, but she felt it had to be brought to light that the government was treating its own citizens this way. She had put herself on the line for her beliefs before, though usually she didn't get arrested. She tended to end up in the hospital. Once, she dislocated some ribs when a falling tree almost crushed her while she was trying to save a grove of old-growth redwoods called Sally Bell. Another time, while she was trying to mediate a dispute, an angry logger punched her in the face and broke her nose.

The guns in the holsters of the men across the road intimidated Mare, but as she stood with the group that had decided to challenge the perimeter, a friend who was a former Marine instructed them to say, "We're nonviolent. We're not going to hurt anybody. We know you're going to arrest us, but we have to cross this line."

As she moved across the road, hands linked with the other protestors, Mare repeated these words over and over.

"We're nonviolent. We're not going to hurt anybody. We know you're going to arrest us, but we have to cross this line."

As soon as Mare ducked under the police line, plastic handcuffs were wrapped around her wrists and she was arrested along with the others. They were placed in a van beyond the trees. Black Hawks thumped overhead, and Mare and the others tried to talk to the young men with guns who were holding them.

"What are you doing here?" she asked. "Why are you being so un-American about it all? Do you think we are Viet Cong or something?"

After darkness fell, the protestors were released.

On the day that Mare and the others were arrested for literally crossing the line, more than three hundred people showed up at the protest. Many had come directly from Reggae on the River, an annual music festival held nearby on the banks of the Eel. Instead of inciting a riot, the crowd turned into a kind of gigantic hippie party.

At one point, a man stood on a makeshift stage next to a "Humboldt Nation" flag, two words that had come to symbolize the apartness and independence of the place where he was standing.

"We're not calling for a revolution," he told the crowd. "We're calling for an end to the war on pot."

In the masses before him, someone held up a giant banner that read, "Legalize Marijuana."

It was probably unimaginable at the time that twenty years later, when it looked like legalization might finally come to pass, it would send tremors of fear through the community.

Later, Rod Deal took to the stage. Deal was Southern Humboldt's Bob Dylan. He was tall and skinny, with Buddy Holly glasses and a black bandito moustache. He strummed his guitar and sang a song called "Marijuana Man."

"I'm an herb smoker. I'm proud to be a marijuana man."

People danced and sang along in front of him, everyone moving to his own beat.

"Things are bad now, but they're gonna be good," Deal sang. "We're gonna know freedom the way that we should."

The citizens of Southern Humboldt weren't the only ones displeased with Operation Green Sweep. Then-Humboldt County sheriff Dave Renner didn't take kindly to how the government had "stormed in" to his county.

"If the Feds have the money for this kind of operation," the sheriff told the *Los Angeles Times*, "they ought to give it to local law enforcement that is more effective and is truly responsible to local citizens. The results speak for themselves, and they are not good."

The results were pretty abysmal. By the time Green Sweep swept out of town, the two-hundred-man operation pulled a total of 1,400 plants. Nobody wanted to officially admit how much Green Sweep had cost the taxpayers, but the National Guard alone spent $400,000, according to *The New York Times*. For contrast, during that same two-week period, twenty members of CAMP, including five sheriff's deputies, destroyed eight thousand plants. As the troops pulled out, the marquee on the Garberville movie theater had a message for them: "Green Sweep U.S.A.—Another $700 Hammer," in reference to the Defense Department scandals of the 1980s, when hundreds of dollars were spent on individual toilets seats and household tools.

———

People continued growing their profitable weed in Humboldt, of course, and contrary to the Bureau of Land Management director's promise, the army and National Guard did not return. Gradually, though, most who grew on public land in those days moved their gardens onto their own property, especially after the passage of the state's medical marijuana law six years later. But the story of Green Sweep and the community's reaction to it speaks to the rebellious nature of the place, and how much things would continue to change in the coming decades as marijuana became increasingly legal. The image of seventeen-year-old Blossom Edwards stumbling upon armed troops would be seared into Humboldt's collective memory forever. What remained largely ignored was how the other children of Humboldt's growers fared.

CHAPTER TEN

Emma

O n a sunny fall morning in 2007, Emma Worldpeace sat in a classroom at the University of California at Berkeley and racked her brain. She was at the start of her senior year at the university and was trying to come up with a subject to write about for a research proposal that was due at the end of the semester.

In her sophomore year, Emma had chosen a major that fit well with her interests, and her last name: peace and conflict studies. In her courses, she learned about wars and genocides, peace movements, and what peace really meant for people—not just the absence of war, but also the existence of harmony and safety, and people having their needs met. Emma's major had an international focus, and for her research proposal she toyed with writing about microfinance in India. But she was also compelled to write about something closer to home. Emma had started to realize that there were many injustices taking place right outside her door.

Maybe I'll write about racial tension in Oakland, she thought. But that didn't feel right, either, and still she couldn't settle on a subject.

On that Berkeley morning, her instructor, a middle-aged woman with cropped brown hair and an elegant air, offered some helpful words.

"It's important to start a research project with a question you have always wanted to know the answer to," she told the class. "If there was something that always seemed a little bit weird, or a little bit wrong, or a little bit off, that nobody has ever given you the answer to, that's probably what you should do your research on."

When Emma heard this, she knew exactly what her question was.

It had been almost four years since she stood before her classmates at South Fork High School at graduation as one of ten co-valedictorians. She loved UC Berkeley and the feeling that there was always something happening on campus, and her fellow students seemed to care about the world and weren't afraid to speak their minds. In her free time, Emma was the captain of the women's cycling team, her relationship with her boyfriend was going steady, and she loved the excitement and stimulation of city life. She enjoyed the cheap Indian restaurants near campus, and the ritual of eating Cheese Board pizza on the grassy median along Shattuck Avenue. One thing she didn't love was how every time she heard a traffic helicopter thump overhead, her blood would run cold for a few scary seconds and she would be reminded of the threat that sound once held in her life.

During her years at Berkeley, Emma didn't hear from her parents very frequently, but every so often, when one of them did ring, she would worry it was because someone else back home had died. If she missed a couple of calls from her mother, she'd wonder, Shit, did my brother die? Did someone close pass away? And sometimes, that would be the case, and Sage would say something like "Oh, did you hear about Maddie and Emily? So tragic."

Madeline "Maddie" Coker and Emily Moody were in Emma's younger sister Lisa's class. In June of 2006, their car went off the road on the way to Shelter Cove and both girls were killed. Lisa called Emma after she got off the phone with her mother, and was very distraught. The girls had all been close friends.

Then, in the summer before Emma's second year of college, Nick LaRue, a friend from Emma's high school class, died in a car accident on the Avenue of the Giants. Her class had been the first at South Fork High to make it from kindergarten to graduation without someone dying. Now, two years out, Nick was gone. Emma thought about it and easily came up with a list of ten people she knew who had died or been murdered in the past five or six years.

Whenever a young person died in Southern Humboldt, people made plastic laminates that were handed out at their memorial. Sean Akselsen's laminate featured a portrait of him taken during high school. He was wearing a black dress shirt and stared at the camera with the handsome, confident gaze of someone whose story was just beginning to unfold. His full name, Sean Thomas Butler Akselsen, was printed along the bottom of the image, along with the dates he entered and left this world. On the other side, superimposed over a painting of Bob Marley, was the poem by Mary Elizabeth Frye that begins, "Do not stand at my grave and weep / I am not there."

People hung these laminates on their rearview mirrors, on bedroom walls, or carried them in their wallets. Emma strung hers on a tackboard on her dorm room wall in Berkeley, alongside cell phone bills and photos from back home. One day a new friend noticed them.

"Did you know all these people who died?" she asked.

"Yeah, I grew up with all of them," Emma replied.

"Oh my God, that seems so tragic."

Her friend had grown up in a rough part of the Bay Area, and Emma was surprised by her reaction.

"Well, you live in a place that's notoriously dangerous. Doesn't this happen to you?" Emma asked.

"Well, sure, maybe every year someone from my school died," her friend said. "But I went to a high school with five or six thousand people."

Emma felt strange about that conversation, and it stayed with her, lingering in the back of her mind. It was her unanswered question.

She waited until after class that morning to run her idea by her instructor.

"In the community I grew up in, there have always been a lot of young people who die," she explained. "I want to know why that happens."

On a Thursday evening in October 2009, Margaret Lewis, the host of a show on KMUD called *Women's Radio Collectively*, announced the theme of the evening's program: growing up in marijuana culture.

"I think it needs some discussion and airing. Not to make any judgments or conclusions," Lewis explained in a deep, professorial tone, "but just to look at what is going on."

The inspiration for the show, she explained, was sparked by a piece that had been performed by a local youth theater company about a family in the growing business with children in high school. In the skit, the children were forced to lie to a career counselor at school about how their parents earned a living. When the daughter in the family wanted to bring a new friend home, the family resisted because there was pot around the house. The family eventually cleaned up their place, and the new friend visited. But while she was there, the Feds conducted a raid and busted the family. The performance left Lewis with the realization that there were unique challenges to growing up in marijuana culture that needed to be addressed.

"I realize that the growing lifestyle is not all negative," she said, giving examples of how neighbors help one another deal with the hazards of the profession such as mold, pests, and law enforcement convoys. But there were unintentional consequences that Lewis wanted to talk about.

"What I would like to discuss here is how we and our children are affected by the duplicity of not being able to openly discuss with new acquaintances, and in some cases family members, our profession, the furtiveness, and the anxiety of possible arrests, and how this lifestyle impacts our families and our lives," she said.

Joining Lewis on the show that evening was a guest and cohost who had become something of an expert on the subject: Emma Worldpeace.

"Thank you for having me, Margaret," Emma told her in a chipper voice.

Emma had brought along three high school students who were also raised in families who grew marijuana. Given that the local industry was still covered in a mantle of secrecy, the young guests, two boys and a girl, remained anonymous, as did the callers to the show, in order to "free up the conversation," as Lewis put it.

Emma had moved back to Humboldt after graduating from Berkeley. She had never intended to return home so quickly, but toward the end of her time in the Bay Area, she realized she missed the peaceful calm that comes with living closer to nature. She had applied for jobs in other states and moved home while she was waiting for something to come through. That something ended up being an AmeriCorps position at the family services center in Redway. In the end, returning to her community was also a way for Emma to share the discoveries she had made during her final semester of school.

"I did my thesis research on death among youth in southern Humboldt County, an issue I think we are all aware of," Emma told listeners that evening. "We have a very high youth death rate, and it's something I had to deal with as a young person, growing up and losing friends, and it's something that we are dealing with now. One of the five emergent themes from my research was basically this, growing up in the marijuana culture."

Emma called this particular theme the "secrecy oxymoron."

During her senior year of college, she attempted to answer that gnawing question about why so many youths in her community died. She sifted data from the county health department and conducted interviews with local teens and adults. In March of that year, Emma presented her thesis to the local school board and a packed public audience at the Garberville Civic Club. Her findings stunned the community: the youth death rate in Southern Humboldt was nearly twice the county average.

From 1994 to 2004, thirty-six youths died in the community in violent or untimely deaths, including car accidents, suicide, and murder. Local youth also had an incredibly high rate of engaging in risky behaviors. Sure, teenagers everywhere take chances, experiment with drugs, and think they are invincible, but Emma found that in Southern Humboldt, the percent of eleventh-graders who had recently engaged in binge drinking was twice the state average, and the number who had recently smoked pot was even higher. These high rates of alcohol and drug use, coupled with frequent reckless driving, lax parental boundaries, and a grim numbness around loss, were themes that emerged during Emma's research.

But on that October evening on KMUD, the focus was on one of the most dominant themes, the one that children in the community had been taught not to talk about. Emma had found it interesting that the marijuana industry was mentioned so often during her interviews about youth deaths.

"Not to say that kids are killed because they are smoking pot, or directly because of it," she explained that night, "but not being able to talk openly about what's going on in your home, or that sense of having a deep fear of law enforcement, can either lead to situations that are very dangerous or prevent you from reaching out for help in an appropriate way when a situation is dangerous."

Lewis, the show's host, had spoken with a friend earlier that day about the topic, and they agreed that not being able to talk about something, be it marijuana or abuse or anything else going on in your house, made it impossible to move past it.

"If you can't talk about it or seek help, there's a stigma about it, and it feels like there is something wrong," Lewis said. "Guests, how do you feel about that?"

The three high school students all agreed and shared stories. The girl admitted that it wasn't fun to hide things from one's friends.

A boy with a husky voice concurred, but said he'd never had that problem.

"You can always tell the kid of a smoker family," he said.

"After a while you know who you can invite over and talk to about these things."

The other boy recalled how during junior high school there was an unspoken agreement among his friends that nobody asked if they could come over during the busy months of harvest season, when pot was dried and cut, and stored at their houses.

"When did you become aware of growing pot and the illegality and what all that meant?" Lewis asked her young guests. "Did you always just know about it or was there a eureka moment?"

When the teenage girl was about eight, her father started bringing her up to the remote piece of land where he grew. She'd smell pot there and occasionally catch glimpses of it, and her father would tell her, "We don't talk about this."

"I never put a second thought to it," she said. "It seemed totally fine."

But when she learned it was illegal, the girl had a different reaction.

"I was so mad at them for it, but over the years now I've had conversations with my parents about it, and they've said they couldn't have the same lifestyle we do if they didn't grow, even if they both had a full-time job."

The second boy grew up in a household where marijuana was, as he put it, very present. As soon as he started school, his parents began to stress that it was something the children couldn't talk about, or they would be taken away.

"It was almost like a daily ritual on the way to school," he said. "They used scare tactics."

The boy with the husky voice had much more relaxed parents, including a mother who liked to belly dance at community events. He got the secrecy talk only after he erroneously told his elementary school teacher that his parents had gone to Las Vegas to get better pot. (They had really gone on a shopping spree.) He was curious why he wasn't allowed to talk about it and discussed the matter with close friends who were in the same position. At that point, he said, he came to a place of acceptance with it.

"Even with it being illegal, it just seemed like the way things were," he said. "Especially in this community, where everyone is doing it."

"Seemingly," Lewis interjected, with a chuckle.

Emma then brought up some of the positive aspects of growing up in pot culture. The way she saw it, the meager amount her mother grew helped supplement the welfare checks she received, put food on the table, and ensured that Emma and her siblings had new shoes. Emma had no memory of being afraid or worrying about it being illegal until her mom got busted.

"It was a complete upset for my entire family," she said.

Sage stopped growing after the bust, and Emma had to find work in her teens, bussing tables after school at a local restaurant. She moved out of the house at sixteen, in part because there wasn't enough money to support her. The hardest part, she remembered, was the secrecy associated with what had happened. She remembered feeling like she couldn't talk to anyone about it and how ashamed she felt.

Returning to the community after spending four years in a vibrant city, Emma now saw everything with different eyes. She looked around at the brilliant young people she went to high school with, who had stayed behind to earn a living growing pot, and she wondered about their futures.

"Sometimes I wonder if that's a genuine choice that they made, or if it's just something that they've fallen into, or if it's something that they've stayed with because they can make a lot of money off of it," she said. "Is there a generation that has been caught up in this that we have lost?"

Lewis, like so many members of the older generation, also wondered about this.

"I've heard young people say I'm just going to grow and make my first million and then I'll go on to school and do all this stuff," she said. "Well, things happen."

Mold happened. Rats happened. Rip-offs happened, she pointed out, and people don't always realize their plans, and then they have to grow for another year, and pretty soon they are caught up in it.

What was more, a man who called into the show pointed out, the children who stayed behind to grow didn't seem to share the values of their elders. Why, he asked, weren't there more young people from the community on the boards of the Mateel, and the Redwoods Rural Health Center, and KMUD, the very radio station the show was being broadcast on? Their parents had built these nonprofit institutions, and for decades supported them with time and money.

The boy with the husky voice had also noticed this. His

theory was that people his age who wanted to help the community and make it a better place were the same people who didn't want to stick around and grow pot.

"Everyone who I've seen in our generation who is saying, 'Hey I can make a lot of money by growing pot,' are the same people who aren't thinking about the community and how they can use that money to help others."

Emma then pointed out the need for more job opportunities in the community so that young people who went away to school could return and put their skills to use.

"This is a beautiful area," she said. "This is an awesome community, there is a lot going on here, but there are no legal jobs."

In an essay in *chronic freedom*, an art book and history of the community that was published in 2010, a writer from the Back-to-the-Land generation makes this very point, after acknowledging that saddling children with the burden of secrecy required them to be dishonest with how they represented themselves to the outside world. "We failed our children by not creating a more broad-based economy in which they could participate if they chose to stay, or left to learn a profession and wanted to return. And in some ways they failed us, those that stayed, by not supporting the institutions we had built. Or is the fact we lost so many children the biggest indictment of all?"

At one point in the conversation, a female listener called in who had just returned from a marijuana legalization conference in San Francisco. The caller had noticed at the conference that most of the harms associated with marijuana were harms of prohibition and the fact that it was illegal, not because of marijuana itself.

"I wonder," the caller said, "what the guests would think if their parents had the same status of a wine grower, who was legal, and they didn't have to hide and worry about it, and what that would mean about all of their choices."

"I would *love* to see it legalized," said Emma. "I think it would make an incredible difference. I think there would be tradeoffs about people not being able to make the kinds of livings that they do off of it now. It would change our relationship with it and make it not so much of a secret we have to carry."

A little over a year later, around the same time that her brother Mike was accused of being involved in a horrible shooting, it seemed as though Emma's wish might come true and that legalization might finally arrive and change that relationship for good.

In the meantime, however, it would be business as usual.

CHAPTER ELEVEN

Bob

B ob Hamilton was in what he called harassment mode. The transient population had been picking up in town, and he felt he was spending way too much of his time dealing with it. A typical interaction went something like this: While cruising down the main drag in Redway, Bob spotted a white Ford Econoline van of 1970s vintage parked in front of the liquor store. It had an old floral-print sheet strung up in the window for curtains, and had clearly seen better days. If the van's engine started, which looked doubtful, it didn't look like it would make it out of town. It was the same white Ford Econoline van that had been parked there all morning.

Bob pulled up alongside the van and picked up the mic that was attached to the public address system on the outside of his car.

"You have to move on," he ordered, his voice booming across the pavement. "You've been parked here too long. This area has a two-hour parking limit."

139

Bob then cruised up to the Mateel Community Center and the Grace Lutheran Church parking lot. On his way back down the hill, he noticed the van hadn't budged an inch.

"God damn it!" Bob swore as he shot across the street and pulled up alongside the Econoline again. This time he hopped out and knocked impatiently on the van's sliding side door until a dazed-looking man emerged. He had long, curly blond hair and a graying beard. He was missing a few of his front teeth and was wearing a faded black T-shirt that read, "I'm Not 50. I'm 18 with 32 Years' Expertise."

"As I already made it clear, you need to move on," Bob told him. "This area has a two-hour parking limit."

The eighteen-year-old with thirty-two years' expertise didn't want to move on.

"I don't have any place to go," he said.

He was also having some health problems.

"Just so you know, the last time, I had a hard time walking from here to the store because my back was out," he told Bob, who didn't appear the least bit interested.

As he pulled away for the second time, Bob breathed a deep sigh and continued down the road, past the sandstone bluffs, toward Garberville. He rolled past the Humboldt House Inn, and the Branding Iron Saloon, which an irate customer once shot up with a machine gun. Across the street, in front of Flavors café, a group of travelers in their early twenties were camped out on the sidewalk with large backpacks.

"You need to move on. No loitering. Pack up your stuff and go." Bob's voice boomed again out of the PA.

As he drove away, he muttered under his breath, "Get a fucking life."

It was that kind of day. Word had finally come in about the budget cuts. As everybody knew, California was broke, and cutbacks were happening everywhere. For the past few months, Bob had been worried that he might either lose his job or end up working security at the county courthouse in Eureka. Things weren't as bad as originally forecast. Bob wouldn't lose his job or end up in the courts, but he was going to have to work twelve-hour shifts. He had pulled long shifts during a previous budget crunch, and knew that they were long and hard, and that, at times, he would be the only deputy on duty and that he'd have to call on Highway Patrol for backup.

After ridding the sidewalks of transients, it was time for Bob to begin working through the pile of arrest warrants stacked on the seat next to him. Outstanding warrants were faxed down from the sheriff's headquarters in Eureka every morning. Most were for people who had been arrested and bailed out and had failed to show up for their court date; people wanted on methamphetamine charges, or for child abductions, or for evading or assaulting a police officer. On top of a pile was a warrant for a twenty-four-year-old man with piercing brown eyes and a goatee who was wanted for drunk driving. The address listed was up a dirt road near Briceland. Bob punched the coordinates into the GPS on his dash, drove a few miles out of town, hung a right, shifted into four-wheel drive, and began a long, slow climb.

Humboldt's dirt roads are infamously rough and labyrinthine, and this one was no exception. Most are un-marked, and many gates don't even have numbers. People who live up the dirt roads have to give directions to visitors that sound straight out of *Winnie-the-Pooh*, such as "Turn left at the gnarled madrone," or "Veer right at the faded prayer flags." If they are particularly courteous, they will escort their visitors to their house the first time they come. The dirt roads seemed made for people to get lost on, especially people with badges in official vehicles.

At one fork, where the road diverged in three directions with no markers, Bob paused for a moment and shook his head.

"Holy smokes, this is like Arkansas. I keep expecting someone from *Deliverance* to come out here and start playing the banjo."

But there were no banjos. Just more dips and turns and dust and locked gates, until the road eventually came to an end. The number on the gate was 840. The number listed on the warrant was 1445. The twenty-four-year-old wanted on drunk driving charges had probably given a fake address. It was often the case.

Bob began to creep slowly back down the hill, with his window open so he could scan the hillside and brush below. Suddenly, he hit the brakes.

"Oh my God!" he shouted. "Look at the size of that fucking greenhouse!"

Through the trees, in the distance, was a greenhouse the size of a small office park. Bob hopped out of the truck, binoculars in hand, to have a clearer look. He could just make out the shadowy shape of marijuana plants on the other side of the papery-white greenhouse walls.

"Plants are tall already," he observed.

Bob had spent the past week eradicating pot plants out in Shelter Cove. He had decided that he wasn't going to deal with marijuana this year because it never led to anything, but then the Shelter Cove Resort Improvement District, the company that provides utility services to the area, had a lawyer draft a letter to the Sheriff's Department requesting assistance dealing with outdoor grows. So Bob spent the past week whacking away at plants that either didn't have 215s posted next to them or were over the county's plant-count limit. Big outdoor grows were an environmental issue to Bob. In an unregulated industry, not all growers were eco-friendly. The chemicals and fertilizers some growers used to encourage plant growth leached into the groundwater and then into the river, where they fed gigantic blue-green algae blooms. Then there was the water itself. Marijuana was a thirsty plant, and many growers pumped so much water from the local rivers in the dry summer months that they reached dangerously low levels.

Bob found it all disgusting. He was still fuming about outdoor grows when the call came in on his cell phone. It was from one of the bounty hunters he had met recently who was trying to track down a fugitive named Keith Conn.

Keith Conn first entered Bob's orbit a few weeks earlier, when he fled from one of Bob's colleagues on Sprowel Creek Road in Garberville. Conn drove a blue Toyota pickup, and he ran a couple of cars off the road as he made his getaway. He was wanted in other California counties on drug and burglary charges, and now he was being sought in Humboldt for evasion. In his Wanted poster back at the station, Keith Conn had ruddy skin and wide, uneasy eyes. He was twenty-nine years old and, in Bob's opinion, a "real bad motherfucker."

The bounty hunters had shown up recently looking for Conn and were now in regular contact with Bob. The one who called had just gotten word that Conn was hiding out in a trailer a few miles up Highway 101. Bob called for backup.

"Phillipsville Loop Road," he said to dispatch.

Then he flipped on his flashing lights, punched on his gas pedal, and raced toward the highway.

Phillipsville Road was located in Phillipsville, a tiny town on the Avenue of the Giants known for its seedy trailer parks, its meth problem, and the Riverwood Inn, a 1930s-era roadhouse and Mexican restaurant that offered live music on the weekends. As Bob raced up the highway at around ninety miles an hour, Deputy Conan Moore shot past him on the left. Conan's cruiser was faster than Bob's Expedition, so the plan was that Conan would go in first, around the back of the road that looped around the town, between the Avenue and the river. Bob would come around the other way, so Keith Conn wouldn't be able to escape.

Just past the town's entrance sign, Bob pulled over to the side of the road, directly across from one of the access points to Phillipsville Road. He sat there hunched over with his hands tightly gripping the wheel, waiting for word from Conan, and entered a kind of trance. His breath was deep and labored, and his gaze was fixed hard on the country lane across the street. After the chase Conn had engaged in with Conan, anything was possible with the man. In a few minutes bullets could even start flying. Should Conn decide to make a break for it, Bob was ready to pounce.

"Are you there yet?" he radioed to his colleague.

"Here."

In a surge of adrenaline, Bob hit the lights and stepped on the gas. His SUV shot across the road. He screeched to a halt a few hundred yards down the lane, next to Conan's cruiser and an old Airstream trailer. Bob had barely stuck his vehicle in Park before he was out the door, popping the snap on the Taser he carried on his right leg as he rushed toward the trailer. He banged loudly on the door.

"Sheriff's Department! Step out and let me see your hands!"

Bob entered the trailer, while Conan waited outside.

Instead of gunfire or screaming, there was only silence.

The aluminum trailer was dented and sagging and looked like a beat-up UFO. A bucket propped up one corner, and it looked like it had been a long time since it had been pulled anywhere on vacation. The property where the trailer was parked was equally run down. There were piles of things under the fruit trees in the yard, and even the light poles couldn't seem to get it together and tilted sadly toward the ground. But like everywhere in Southern Humboldt, natural beauty wasn't far. Across the street was a grassy meadow where horses ran free, and in almost every direction were tree-studded hills.

Bob emerged from the trailer with a woman in handcuffs. He sat her down on a broken porch swing outside. She was skinny, with bleached hair and a worried face. She shared a name with the disgraced figure skater Tonya Harding. A few minutes later Bob brought an older man with a white beard to join her. He was barefoot and shirtless; a metal chain ran from the belt loop of his jeans to the wallet in his pocket, where his ID revealed he was sixty-four. Behind a ratty camouflage tarp in one corner of the yard was a scrawny 215 medical pot garden, but Keith Conn was nowhere to be found. When Bob was done searching the trailer, he uncuffed the couple and let them go.

Bob sighed when he got back in the Expedition. It felt like he'd been chasing Conn forever, and he would have lived for a month off the high of catching him.

He called in the news to the bounty hunter in Sacramento.

"He wasn't there," he said. "But there was a woman named Tonya Harding."

There was a pause.

"No, not that one."

The bounty hunter offered up one more tip: Conn might be with his girlfriend, a woman who went by the name of Brandy Land, who was staying at the Lone Pine Motel in Garberville.

"Lone Pine, number nine," Bob told Conan, as they got back in their vehicles and headed toward Garberville.

Driving back down the 101 toward town, Bob felt let down, but part of him still hoped he might find Conn in the motel room. He wanted to catch him so bad, he could feel the adrenaline coursing through his veins.

The Lone Pine Motel was located on Main Street directly across from Ray's Food Place. Rooms started at sixty dollars a night and, according to a sign out front, included free wireless "enternet" and use of the pool. Contrary to what the name of the motel seemed to suggest, there was no pine tree towering over the place. A redwood tree used to grow in the parking lot, until it became the casualty of a severe storm that past winter. A local chain saw artist carved what was left of the stump into a kind of feline sculpture that Bob referred to as "the kitty."

Room number nine was located next to the street. Conan went around to knock and see if anyone was inside, while Bob stood guard on the sidewalk to make sure no one popped out of any windows. A few minutes later, Conan strolled back around the side of the building empty-handed. He looked at Bob and shrugged. Bob scrunched up his face and pretended to cry.

It was nearly the end of the day when the last call came in. A local businesswoman asked Bob to meet her at the auto parts store across from the Laundromat. She had short brown hair and a stocky build. She pulled Bob aside and gave him the name of a guy she said was involved in high-level pot trafficking with people from LA.

The house was located near the ACE hardware store in Garberville. A beat-up twenty-year-old Honda Accord was parked out front, next to some garbage bags and old car seats. A short wooden gate sealed the entrance to the yard.

Standing in front of it, Bob had a full view of a small crop of three-foot-tall marijuana plants. A heavyset man sitting in the yard saw Bob and walked up to the gate.

"Do you have a Two-fifteen?" Bob asked him. "For this law to work, if you have marijuana, you gotta have a Two-fifteen. If it's here and there's not a Two-fifteen, I gotta yank it."

"I'm growing for my sister who lives out in Briceland," said the man, who identified himself as Edward. "She has a Two-fifteen."

Bob entered the long, rectangular yard. There were a few trees and rosebushes sprouting up around it; the small plot of pot plants was near the back fence. The house was a one-story and pistachio green. A large heap of trash, or perhaps storage, was piled under a tarp to the right of the front door.

Bob looked at Edward.

"It has to be here when I show up. If there's no Two-fifteen posted, I have to consciously believe it's an illegal grow," he said. "It's on your property, and I have to assume it's yours. That's what we're up against. How many plants are there? Twenty-nine? Twenty-one?"

Before Edward could answer, Deputy Conan Moore showed up at the gate.

"There's a grow here and there's no Two-fifteen," Bob called out to him.

Then a woman emerged from the house. She was wearing jeans and flip-flops; large silver hoops dangled from her ears. She had been in the middle of coloring her hair when Bob arrived, and it was piled on top of her head in a dark, wet coil.

"Aren't there cases where you give someone more time to get one?" she asked.

"I used to do that, but not anymore," Bob replied.

"So, what, we have to unplant them and then replant them?" The woman started to tremble and cry. "This is helping us," she said, her voice cracking. "Is there any way you could possibly let me call her and bring it over?"

Bob called the sister in Briceland. It turned out that she did have a 215, but she needed it for her garden. These plants, it seemed, were doomed to be pulled.

"How many are there?" Bob asked Conan.

"I counted fifty-nine," he said.

Most were in the ground, and about eight or so were sitting in pots on top of a plastic pickle barrel near the gate. Planted among the pot plants were some tomato plants, lettuce, and a tiny strawberry patch. Everything looked in need of a good watering.

Bob was frustrated.

"It's simple, simple rules. You grow marijuana, you have a Two-fifteen. We're going to take the grow and I'm going to cite you both," he told the couple. "I won't arrest you and take you north, but there is a big lesson here. I'm very lenient when it comes to marijuana, but you have to have a Two-fifteen."

The woman sobbed as Conan walked among the plants and took pictures of them. He then snapped on a pair of blue plastic gloves and picked up a small machete. Conan had been with the Sheriff's Department for only a few years and had recently transferred to Garberville from the Hoopa substation, which was located near the Hoopa Valley Indian Reservation, the largest reservation in the state. He was stocky, with a thick brown moustache and a bit of a paunch. He had the kind of sturdy build that would have made for a good logger, in another lifetime.

Pulling out the grow took a matter of minutes. Conan grabbed each plant by the stalk, bent it, and gave it a good whack with the machete, which made a dull *thwap* as it cut through the fibrous stalk.

"Could you please leave the tomatoes?" the tearful woman called out from the porch.

He did. When he was finished, Conan stacked all the plants in the back of Bob's SUV and scraped the blade of the machete clean on the edge of a plastic pickle barrel that was sitting in the yard.

"So if I get my own Two-fifteen and it's posted, would I be able to replant?" the woman asked.

"Of course," said Bob, as he began to read her husband his Miranda rights.

On his way out, Bob shook his head. "I could have cared less if they were over the limit. We don't care about numbers anymore as long as they have a Two-fifteen. So there's just no excuse for it."

He headed back to the substation to do the paperwork. Somewhere, out among the trees, Keith Conn was waiting for him. Beyond that, there were more marijuana plants than he could ever count or chop down, inching slowly toward harvest.

CHAPTER TWELVE

Mare

The plants in the greenhouse had grown big and tall, and into the names Mare Abidon had given them. Mare christened the six plants she grew every year, and in the fall of 2010, a tall *sativa* named Willow stood toward the back. Willow towered over the other plants, her long, stacked flower clusters, or colas, as long as Mare's forearm and practically scraping against the twelve-foot-high greenhouse ceiling. Next to Willow stood Red Haired Beauty, Petey, and Big Bertha, the name Mare bestowed every year on her largest, roundest plant. Outside the greenhouse, next to an old solar panel, Mare grew her other two plants.

After endless months of watering, staking, and attention, it was finally harvest time, and perhaps the final one before marijuana was fully legal. Dressed in white overalls and armed with a pair of clippers, Mare began snipping off the top colas and stacking them gently in the Indian rice basket at her feet. The idea was that by clipping off the top buds, whose hairs had already started to turn brown and were ready for harvest, the smaller flower clusters underneath would be exposed to more light and would reach maturity faster.

Earlier in the year—around the same time Mare was getting excited about the "What's After Pot?" meeting, and when semis loaded with marijuana soil were beginning their annual roll through town—a man named Jim had started these plants. First, he took the tiny speckled seeds and wrapped them in a damp paper towel, which he then placed somewhere warm. Within a week, when tiny white shoots poked through the seed casings, he gently pressed them into a tray of moist earth. Soon, little green leaves appeared, first two, and then four, and like tiny green butterflies, they began their long reach for the sun.

Mare and Jim had known each other since the 1970s. He now lived on Mare's property and worked as her pot "partner," helping with the crop in exchange for rent. There was another man, a younger guy named William, who also lived on the property, in a similar arrangement. He helped Mare with firewood and other manual chores. Mare always thought she'd end up on a women's commune, but somehow she'd ended up surrounded by men.

Growing from seed was the old Humboldt way. Most new and industrial-scale growers grew from clones, which were clippings from a female plant. Just as a slip of a geranium will produce the same colored flowers and lemony-rose scent of the plant it was taken from, a branch of a female marijuana plant will grow to possess the same qualities of its "mother." Growing from clones eliminated the guesswork involved with pot growing, and saved time and energy for growers who didn't want to bother having to throw out half their crop once the plants revealed their sex, or risk seeding their crop if they failed to detect a male before he released pollen into the air.

Mare had tried growing from clones once, about ten years earlier, and she didn't care for it. It didn't seem natural. It was like the difference between using chemicals or compost for fertilizer. Growing pot to Mare was a process where every year it was different; you never knew what you were going to get. It was about alchemy. Mare found clones rather dull. The year she grew with them, all her plants were females and they were exactly alike; it was like they all had the same name. Clones seemed so automatic, which was the point, but growing so that everything was identical didn't appeal to Mare. It was like the difference between monoculture and diversity.

Some of the seeds used to grow Willow, Big Bertha, and the others had an unusual provenance. While on a recent art tour of Europe with an old friend, Mare had stopped by the Sensi Seed Bank in Amsterdam. She was hoping to buy some pure *sativa* seeds. Mare had been growing *sativas* since the early days. It was her specialty. She called it "lady dope" because it produced a light, cerebral high that she and her female artist friends favored because it seemed to inspire creativity. In the beginning, of course, everyone grew *sativas* because the pot they smoked came from Mexico and Colombia, where *sativas* flourished, and before *sinsemilla*, they just plucked out the seeds that came with their stash and planted them in the garden. Then, in the late 1970s, a few cunning couriers brought *indica* seeds back from Asia. Mare credited the Vietnam vets with bringing *indica* home with them, but then there were also people from the community who traveled east on a very specific mission, like the man from Southern Humboldt who called himself Douglas Fir.

In 1978, a year before the Soviet invasion, Douglas Fir landed in Afghanistan. He then proceeded to smoke hash and play badminton at a house in Kabul, while a messenger was dispatched into the mountains of the Hindu Kush. The messenger returned with *indica* seeds, which Douglas Fir brought back to Humboldt sewn in the hems and cuffs of his clothing. The short plants the seeds produced reached maturity quicker than *sativas*, and their high was intoxicatingly strong. Over the years, *indica* seeds were crossbred with *sativas* in thousands of wacky-named combinations, producing a super-strong, THC-heavy high. The first time Mare ever smoked *indica*, it felt as if her knees were melting under her. There was even a word among pot smokers to describe the kind of catatonic high *indica* could produce: *couch lock*.

As pure *sativas* fell out of favor, Mare stockpiled seeds from friends, but the strain she grew was weak, since a seed stock could continue for only so long. Since *sativas* had become so rare, and it was illegal to buy marijuana seeds in the United States, she figured she'd stock up in famously liberal Holland.

When Mare reached the counter at the Sensi Seed Bank in Amsterdam, she requested a pure *sativa*.

"You might want to try something else," the man who was helping her suggested. "*Sativas* are really difficult for beginners."

Mare snorted. "Who do you think started all of this?" she asked.

The interaction was the first inkling Mare had that something had changed while she was living her bliss in the woods.

The man behind the counter had no idea that the indignant older woman in front of him had been growing pot since before he was born, but he put her in touch with the local seed guru. The guru, it turned out, was also from California. Though it is a federal felony to bring marijuana seeds into the country, as a white, elderly hippie, Mare clearly didn't fit the profile of the modern-day drug mule. When she returned home, hidden in her luggage, inside a half-eaten box of chocolate nibs, were a handful of seeds called Jumping Jack Flash. Hidden inside Mare herself, in her "orifice," was a strain called Bubble Gum.

———

It was these very seeds that were crossed with another strain that produced the plant Mare had begun to harvest. When her basket was full of musky, sticky flowers, she turned around and walked back toward the cabin she referred to as her favorite art project. Mare had designed the building in 1980, with the help of a passive solar living handbook. It was exactly as you'd imagine a cabin in the woods: surrounded by mossy trees, no signs of civilization in sight, and a model of self-sufficiency and sustainability. Water came from a nearby stream, heat from the woodstove, and electricity from the solar panels near the greenhouse. Mare's only utility bill was for the natural gas she used to cook and sometimes heat her water.

She pulled open the sliding glass door and entered the main living space, which was always bright and airy no matter what the season, thanks to the six enormous windows that made up the entire south-facing wall. Mare shuffled past the jumble of blankets and pillows that covered her bed. Beyond it were stairs that led to the loft where she dried her pot and herbs, and the small woodstove, which she kept burning steadily throughout the harvest to ensure that her plants dried at an even temperature. Feathers and crystals hung from the window above the kitchen sink, which looked out on the tree line.

To say that the compact space was cluttered would be a severe understatement. As she made her way toward the stairs, Mare had to step over a pair of fuzzy black slippers, and a layer of pine needles, dog hair, branches, and other debris. An old vacuum cleaner was parked next to a stack of *National Geographic*s, and it had clearly not been fired up in a while.

Every nook and cranny in the room seemed to be overflowing with relics from Mare's past. Among the contents hemorrhaging from under the stairs, for instance, were a book on herbology, an illustrated poster of wild mushrooms, some old cassette tapes, an empty bag of organic blue corn tortilla chips, pink spray paint, and a box of Georgia O'Keeffe note cards.

Mare was well aware of her housekeeping skills, or lack thereof. Her whole philosophy on the subject was summed up in the A. A. Milne quote she'd tacked up next to her back porch door: "One of the advantages of being disorderly is that one is constantly making exciting discoveries." Mare had considered making copies of the quote and handing them out to her friends, so that instead of cleaning their houses, they could just put up the sign, too, but she'd never gotten around to it.

Mare was famous among her friends for her banking system, which was a direct result of her disorderliness. Living in a cash economy, where to store your money is always an issue. The old-school Humboldt way was to bury it in your yard or deep in the woods, in plastic pickle barrels or glass Mason jars. This led to many stories about people who buried their savings and weren't able to find them again, or who came across a cache of cash while landscaping a new backyard. Mare didn't bury her money so much as lose it by accident. Things even disappeared on her person. Once, she bought cashier's checks at the post office and put them in her shoe for safekeeping. She then proceeded to forget about them. She looked everywhere for those checks, until one day she felt a lump in her shoe and discovered the valuable clump of worn-down paper. She used to hire her friends' daughters to search her house for money. She'd pay them a 25 percent finder's fee.

It was warm up in the loft. Mare had sealed off the far end with white and pink sheets, which she had tacked to the ceiling and draped on the floor. She peeled back the cloth and stepped inside her drying area. String was pulled tight across the ceiling in neat rows, to be used for hanging the buds. A few were already in the process of drying, infusing the space with a sweet, skunky smell. She began clumping together the smaller buds in the basket and attaching rubber bands around their stems. Even though it was damp out at the coast, Mare didn't have a problem with mold or mildew that year like Crockett did. She then attached paper clips to the bundles of buds, bent them into little hooks, and hung them from the string above.

After three days or so, when the outside leaves of pot had grown brittle to the touch, Mare would wrap paper bags around the branches while they were still hanging. She would then check on them daily, until the stems cracked when she applied a little pressure. When this happened, they were ready, and she would carefully place the dried flowers in paper bags for around two weeks of curing. Then she would wrap the paper bags up tight and place them in a black plastic garbage bag, which she would store somewhere cool and dark until she had a buyer. Unlike most growers, Mare didn't trim her marijuana right after harvest. She used an old herbalist's trick, leaving the outer leaves to form a protective barrier over the buds while they dried, which provided a cushion and helped preserve their scent during storage.

Mare wiped her hands on her overalls, stood back, and surveyed her work. Though she had been hanging pot in her loft for years, she had made some new additions to the space this fall, specifically the sheets that enclosed the area. The blinds were pulled shut, but the sun seeped around the edges and through the pink material, casting a rose glow and giving the enclosure a womblike feeling.

But the idea behind the sheets wasn't about atmosphere; it was about sanitation and creating a dust-free environment. In the old days, a little cat or dog hair on pot was proof that it was homegrown, but Mare had recently joined a collective, and this clean drying space was one of the membership requirements.

Not long after the "What's After Pot?" event, a local couple held a meeting at the Octagon at Beginnings in Briceland, the place for community gatherings of all kinds. At the meeting, the couple announced that they were going to form a collective under the state's medical model, to provide patients in the Bay Area with good, old-fashioned Humboldt medicine, grown the traditional way: organically, under the sun, by farmers who had been doing it that way since the very beginning. They called it the Tea House Collective, and their target patient was the discriminating Whole Foods shopper. Anyone interested in joining the collective had to be a medical grower, pay $1,500, and donate a pound of pot. In exchange, everyone in attendance was told, the collective would try to sell their marijuana legally to patients for $2,800 a pound, which was a nice price.

Mare didn't make that first meeting, but she heard about

it from her neighbors and thought the collective would be the way to get her pot to patients legally. She had been growing medically for years. Her 215 was for her asthma and her arthritis. Recently, though, it had been harder and harder to sell her crop. Mare still had two pounds from the previous year in storage that she had been unable to find a market for. Old college friends who used to buy from her in the Bay Area had started to die off, or had begun to go to the dispensary down the street when their stash ran out. The Tea House sounded like the wave of the future, and a way to be legal and out in the open whether or not the legalization measure passed in November.

In turning in her application, membership fee, and pound of pot, Mare joined a group of some two dozen others who wanted to go legit. Many were seniors, like her, fellow Back-to-the-Landers who were now in their sixties and seventies. They included a folk musician with a white beard and twinkly eyes who used to live in the West Village and had once played guitar with Peter, Paul, and Mary. He was joined by his fortysomething son, a second-generation grower. Other members included a Prius-driving grandmother whose ninety-one-year-old mother sometimes helped trim her pot, a former art school professor from Chicago, a woman from Hawaii who'd ended up in Humboldt by accident thirty years earlier, and an environmentalist from Minnesota who had helped save vast swaths of alerce forest in Chile. As the Prius-driving grandmother put it, they were, for the most part, "old-growth growers."

Members of the collective underwent a quality control

to make sure they grew outdoors without chemicals, helped preserve the fish populations by not pumping water from local rivers during the summer months, and kept their processing facilities clean. It was an attempt to self-regulate a still-unregulated industry. A man came around to inspect Mare's scene, to make sure she met the standards of her collective. When he saw all the untreated wood on the walls, ceiling, and floor of her loft, he told her she would have to sand and seal it. Then he called her back later and suggested that maybe she should rent a special drying shed in town. It felt so complicated that Mare called one of the founders in tears and offered to drop out of the collective, but the founder came up with the compromise of sealing off the space with sheets to create a sterile area, and that seemed to satisfy everyone.

So much had changed since the old days. Back then, all sizes of buds went in the same bag; now they were sorted according to size and grade. When Mare used to find mold on a bud, she'd take it out, but what was next to it—which probably had mold spores on it, too—would be sold. Now, with most dispensaries requiring lab testing for mold, Mare realized it wasn't good for people with compromised immune systems who smoked pot as their medicine. The industry was changing fast.

Then there was the difference between indoor- and outdoor-grown pot. Over the years, Mare had somehow been oblivious to the rising popularity of marijuana grown inside under high-intensity lights. During the heavy and hard years of CAMP, some growers had moved indoors to avoid detection, but Mare didn't realize how prolific indoor growing had become, or how valuable, until she took a trip to Harbin Hot Springs with a few of her girlfriends. Harbin was a clothing-optional New Age retreat in nearby Lake County. While Mare and her friends were in the area, they decided to pay a visit to the nearby pot dispensary. Most of the ladies had been growing pot for decades but had never visited an actual pot store before. Though there were already more dispensaries in California than there were Starbucks or McDonald's, there wasn't yet a single one in Southern Humboldt.

The women were in for an awful shock.

At the Lake County dispensary, as at those throughout the state, the kind of organic, sun-grown marijuana they grew was considered bottom of the market. The dispensary was selling it for thirty dollars for an eighth of an ounce. The kind of pot Crockett grew—outside, in a greenhouse—was going for sixty dollars an eighth, and pot grown inside was selling for ninety dollars an eighth. The women were ap-palled. It was as if organic heirloom tomatoes or free-range eggs were worth less than some mass-produced factory version.

One of Mare's friends asked the reason behind the pric-ing. She was told it was because wind could blow debris on marijuana grown outdoors and it was considered kind of dirty. It was also less expensive to grow in the sun, they were told, and the pot it produced tended to be less potent than the average indoor crop, which was untrue.

The women left feeling dejected.

In the past seven months since her official coming-out as a pot grower, things hadn't turned out well for Mare. She had never expected pot would be illegal for so long, but now that it was almost legal, she felt invisible. It reminded her of that interaction she had at the seed bank in Amsterdam. She had recently come across a glossy magazine called *Rosebud*, which billed itself as a "hydroponics lifestyle" publication. Celebrities graced its cover, and inside were ads for $24,000 computerized hydroponic systems. There was no mention of outdoor growing anywhere in the magazine. It was starting to seem like only old hippies grew pot under the sun. Indoors was slick, young, and lucrative. It was dismaying to Mare that marijuana had become such a commodity. She felt like something important was being forgotten.

Mare hung the last of her buds to dry and prepared to make another trip to the greenhouse. She thought again that if legalization didn't happen, and the Tea House Collective didn't work, it might just be time to think about retirement.

Elsewhere in Humboldt, a grower sitting in jail faced an even bigger problem.

CHAPTER THIRTEEN

Emma

A week after learning about the shooting Mike was allegedly involved in, Emma Worldpeace started up her black Subaru Impreza and began the four-hour drive from Chico back to Humboldt. She drove down a busy I-5, the interstate that bisects California, and then through oak forest and farmland on a tiny state route, before connecting with Highway 101 in Mendocino County, and pushing north, back behind the redwood curtain. Emma was on her way to meet both of her sisters at Aia's house in Eureka. The girls were going to get together and talk about what had happened with Mike, who was sitting downtown in the Humboldt County jail charged with murder, attempted murder, and marijuana cultivation.

The weekend after she learned about the shooting, Emma and her boyfriend, Ethan, had been riding through Chico on their bikes when a friend drove by them and stopped to say hello.

"Hey, did you hear about that shooting that went on in Humboldt?" the friend asked. They knew that Emma was originally from there.

Emma got a huge lump in her throat and wanted to tear up. She was unable to say, "Yes, that was my brother."

Emma hadn't seen much of Mike in recent years, and when she did, it was painfully obvious that they inhabited different worlds. When Emma was at Berkeley, Mike used to tease her about how broke she was, and how spending thousands of dollars on her education was a major waste of money. Here he was, she remembered him telling her, making $100,000 a year growing pot. He had just bought his own home, and he hadn't even graduated from high school.

During her junior year at Berkeley, Emma went up to visit Mike and her older sister, Aia, who was living with him at the time. It was Halloween, and as the girls were putting the finishing touches on their costumes and preparing to go out for the evening, Emma started talking about a class she was taking that she was excited about. She expected Mike to shoot it down as usual, but instead, he listened and looked thoughtful. It was as though something inside him had changed. At twenty-six, he was now struggling to make his loan payments on his house. He'd never had a legal job and didn't really have anything to show for all his hard work that wasn't fake or made up in some way.

Following Mike's arrest, Aia took in his pit bulls, Alou and Lola. Emma always found them to be sweet, nice dogs, but they had been pepper-sprayed by the authorities, and for six days after Aia picked them up, they were unable to eat and were edgy and would bark aggressively at anyone who came to the door. Lisa knew the dogs well; she had lived with Mike most recently, and knew what food to buy for them and how to get them to eat again.

The sisters gathered around a laptop in Aia's living room and pored over the coverage of the shooting. In the days following Mike's arrest, more news had come out about the incident. In a bizarre coincidence, it turned out that Humboldt County sheriff's deputies had already been investigating Mike and were in the process of preparing a warrant to search his property on the morning of the shooting. His garden was big enough to attract attention during a sheriff's helicopter flyover.

The sisters clicked through the news coverage and were shocked by some of the readers' comments. Some made fun of the hippie spelling of Mike's name. Others called for his blood. "He deserves nothing more than a bullet in the back of his head, and to be hung from a tree for vultures to eat," wrote one reader on a Mendocino news site.

Most sickening to Emma was the racism toward the Guatemalan men who had been shot.

"How come no one's saying anything about these guys being illegal immigrants?" asked a commenter at *The North Coast Journal*, as if the men's immigration status had anything to do with their being shot.

"What were these men doing in Humboldt County?" asked another.

Eventually the sisters just had to stop reading. It was too upsetting.

Sometimes Emma would go back and forth between calling Mike her stepbrother or her brother, but the truth was that she loved and cared about him as a brother. She didn't want him to rot in jail, but if he did shoot those men in cold blood, she knew that justice needed to be served.

On her long drive back to Chico a few days later, Emma reflected on everything that had happened. She thought about the legalization measure, and how excited she had been when she first heard about it. She always thought that pot should be legal, especially when compared with alcohol. It just made sense. If pot were legal, sure, there would be less money in the black market, but the region would adjust eventually and then there would be less fear and shame in the community, and greater tax revenue for the schools. Not to mention that business-related violence would come to an end, just like it had at the end of alcohol prohibition.

Emma was still living in Humboldt when the news broke about the upcoming legalization vote, and she heard the undercurrent of opposition in the community from people who were scared it would threaten their economic security. She also knew people who were preparing to adapt, like her best friend's mother, whom she rented a room from at the time. The woman grew a few plants in a spare room to supplement her full-time work at the local health food store. She told Emma that she thought maybe she'd rent out the room to make up for the loss in income after legalization. Throughout the summer, the measure was ahead in the polls, and looked pretty inevitable.

After a yearlong courtship, Emma had moved to Chico

that spring to live with Ethan. The couple had met through the cycling community, and shared a mutual love of the sport. Emma hoped to get into graduate school in Chico and study social work, but in the meantime, she found a job at the bike shop.

The couple thought about maybe returning to Humboldt together someday. Ethan loved the natural beauty of the area and would move there in a heartbeat if he could find a decent job that wasn't in the marijuana industry. Emma had her doubts. She so loved the place and thought about how fulfilling it would be to be a counselor at her old high school, to be able to talk to kids about their situations, and to have her own children attend the same sweet hippie schools she once did. But then she'd return home over the summer to visit, and she'd see all these strange, shady people in town, people drawn to the area not for the community, but to grow and make money and live as outlaws. She'd read about all the spooky crimes in the local paper, and she'd recall all the sad-ass stories of her youth and she'd have second thoughts about moving back. Maybe it wouldn't be such a great place to start a family. Or maybe if pot did become legal, it would even the playing field, and the people who lived in Humboldt would be there because they loved the place and wanted to participate in the community, and not just because they wanted to benefit from the pot economy.

Then this thing with Mike happened, and Emma was reminded once again that people were killed over pot. She was just so ready for the drama, and the violence, and the excessiveness to end. If she held out any hope for the situation, it was that others would learn from Mike's story, that he would serve as a kind of cautionary tale. So many of the boys she grew up with had just stayed and grown pot, and seemed headed in the same direction as Mike. Emma had heard so many people say that if someone stepped on their property and tried to steal their shit, they would shoot the person. Emma thought that kind of behavior needed to be condemned. She didn't think that was what her parents and the hippie settlers who stumbled across pot as a way to make money and support their families would have wanted. The hope for most people was that it never got to the point where they had to pull a trigger, but maybe if Mike were found guilty, his story would serve as a reminder that if you took someone else's life, you were taking your own life in a way, too.

The men who were shot in Mike's garden were people with families who loved them, people who had had hopes and dreams of their own. It was Emma's wish that the fact the men were undocumented immigrants from another country wouldn't lessen Mike's punishment if he were found guilty, because that would be valuing one type of human life over another, and that, she thought, would be disgusting.

Little did she know that the vote and what happened afterward would delay the justice process in Mike's case for a long time to come.

CHAPTER FOURTEEN

Bob

J ust past ten o'clock one fall morning, when the leaves on the alder trees had started to turn yellow and shadows had begun to fall longer on the ground, Bob Hamilton rocketed down the Avenue of the Giants. The trees and river passed by in a foggy green blur. He hung a hard left onto Phillipsville Road, the same road he had raced down a few months earlier in search of the fugitive Keith Conn. This time he shot past the beat-up Airstream where he once thought Conn was hiding out and swung a right, toward a house filled with sadness.

A woman had died. She'd had lupus, Bob was told, and was under a Do Not Resuscitate (DNR) order so she could die from natural causes. Normally, Bob wouldn't have responded to a call about someone under such an order, but the deceased woman's daughter had called him on his cell phone a few minutes earlier and told him she suspected that drugs might be involved. Not only was Humboldt County home to nearly half of the planet's remaining old-growth red-woods and the longest undeveloped stretch of coastline in California, but in 2010, Humboldt also had the distinction of having the state's highest drug-induced death rate. Of course none of these deaths was due to marijuana, which no one has ever died from overdosing on. But like many poor, rural counties, Humboldt had a high rate of death from methadone, methamphetamine, and prescription drugs such as Vicodin and Oxycontin.

Bob pulled to a stop in front of a two-story house with a sagging front porch. The young woman who had called him was waiting by the side of the road. She had long brown hair and was dressed in the kind of clothes you throw on when you're awoken by a phone call with bad news: a hoodie, sweat pants, and Ugg boots. In her arms she held a small blond boy in Space Invader pajamas. A man in a base-ball cap hovered protectively nearby. The woman's face was tearstained, and her voice cracked as she greeted Bob.

"I want to know if drugs were involved and if she OD'd on something," she said. "I want to know if she did it herself or not..."

The woman's voice trailed off and she began to weep. The man standing next to her wrapped his arm around her shoulder, and an older woman appeared out of nowhere to scoop the child out of her arms.

Bob had met the couple once before, in an enormous greenhouse full of pot. The little boy was just a baby then. They didn't have a 215, so it was an illegal grow. The couple told Bob that they were trying to get money to build a house.

He arrested the man, but only cited the woman because of the baby in her arms. Even though they had been busted, something about Bob's interaction with the couple must have earned him their respect, because when the woman learned her mother had died, she called Bob almost immediately.

Bob pulled a small notebook and a pen out of his front pocket and began his police work. The young woman was named Kayla. She was twenty-two. Her mother, the deceased, was Christina. She was born in December 1964, and had died that morning in the room she rented in a house a few feet from where they were standing. For much of her life, Christina had battled heroin addiction.

Bob turned toward the house. It was large and rambling, and overlooked the South Fork of the Eel River in the back. Like most places in Phillipsville, it looked as though its heyday had been back around the time of the logging boom. Bob stepped into the front yard and realized that he had been there before. He had once kicked down the front gate while chasing a suspect.

In the hallway inside, a skinny woman with blond hair and the raspy voice of someone who smoked too many cigarettes was speaking to a woman who turned out to be the deceased's sister. The blonde's name was Cinderella, but everybody called her Cindra.

Bob glanced around the corner to the kitchen and an enormous living room beyond. Oriental carpets covered the floors, along with four overstuffed couches and a pool table. The place smelled musty, as if no one had opened the windows in a very long time.

"How long has she lived here?" he asked.

"I'm guessing six months," said Cindra. "Some days she was pretty decent; other days she was in so much pain she couldn't move."

A man with long white hair and a white beard, who looked a little bit like Gandalf the Grey, passed by. His name was Steven and he owned the house. Steven was barefoot, and seemed oblivious to the chill in the air in shorts and a T-shirt. He appeared disturbed by the morning's events and unable to stop pacing. Bob had heard of Steven before but couldn't remember why. It wouldn't be long before he heard about Steven again. In retrospect, all Steven's pacing that morning might have been simple discomfort at having Bob poking about his house.

In the kitchen, next to a garbage can full of empty liquor bottles and a sliding glass door that looked out onto the swollen river outside, Bob learned the story of Christina's death from the man who had found her. Ron rented the bedroom across the hall. He had buzzed white hair, and his eyes were wet with tears.

As Bob scribbled the story in his tiny notebook, Ron explained that the previous day had been a bad one for Christina. The chronic inflammation associated with lupus had made her hands ache, and her caregiver had tried to soothe the pain with an injection in her back.

At around 8:30 that morning, Ron went to check on Christina and was greeted by an eerie stillness.

"I could tell from the second I opened the door she was gone," Ron said.

Out on the front porch, Kayla, Christina's daughter, was crying.

"I'm sorry for overreacting," she said as Bob walked up to her. He gently wrapped his arm around her shoulder.

"You're not overreacting," he told her. "Your mom passed away."

After interviewing Cindra, the only person left to see was Christina herself. Her bedroom was located in an alcove at the top of the stairs. She was lying on a double bed that was pushed up against the window. Bob peeled back the red-and-white-check afghan that covered her. Christina had dark hair and pale, waxy skin. She looked gaunt, and her jaw was frozen open. As he peered down at her, Bob realized that, like the house and so many of the people in it, he had history with Christina, too. She had sold heroin out of a place she used to rent in Redway. Bob quietly pulled the afghan back over her head.

The night table next to her was littered with prescription pill bottles. Bob glanced at their labels. There were enough little orange bottles to fill a paper grocery bag. On the windowsill above the bed was a framed photograph of an attractive young woman in her thirties, with a young girl seated next to her. It was Christina and Kayla in happier times.

Downstairs, on one of the overstuffed couches in the living room, Bob delivered his findings to Kayla.

"There's no reason for me to believe there was any foul play," he told her. "I just wanted you to know what I came up with and that I'm really sorry for your loss."

Upstairs, Bob gathered up a box of jewelry, Christina's purse, cell phone, and a few other personal effects for Kayla. Kayla's husband grabbed the framed portrait above the bed.

"One of the saddest things when my mom died is that I had nothing of hers," Bob said as he handed the things over, and remembered the death of his own mother in a fire all those years ago.

"If you need me, call me," he told Kayla as he walked out the door. Employees from a funeral home in Fortuna were on their way to collect the body.

"Thanks, Hamilton."

Bob rubbed sanitizer over his hands as he drove away. Deathwise, it was all very short and sweet. On the drive back toward 101, yellow alder leaves were scattered across the roadway in front of him. Later on during his patrol that day, Bob's mind would wander to the less sweet stories from his years in law enforcement and the things he'd seen that would forever haunt him, like the five-year-old boy who was accidentally shot and killed by his father on a hunting trip. Bob had had to scoop the lifeless child out of the car that day, and he would never forget how his tiny body felt like a bag of chicken bones and Jell-O in his arms.

Then there was the nine-year-old girl he hit after she Rollerbladed out in front of his squad car one evening in Fresno. After a brief hospital stay, she ended up being fine, but Bob was so distraught by the guilt and the memory of the girl crumpling to the ground in front of his car that he had to take time off from work.

More recently, a Humboldt woman out in Whitethorn had tried to take her life in a particularly horrific way. She was wielding a butcher knife when Bob arrived at her house. Her response to his command to drop it was to race into a bedroom and lock the door. After hearing strange gurgling sounds coming from the other side of the door, Bob kicked the door down and discovered the woman had slit her throat. She then tried to fight him off as Bob applied pressure to her wounds with his bare hands. There was so much blood his sleeves were soaked up to his elbows. Bob later received life-saving awards from both the Red Cross and the Sheriff's Department for his actions. The woman lived, thanks to him, but would go on to attempt suicide again.

After all he had seen, it was no wonder to Bob that police officers had such a high rate of suicide, almost twice that of the general population. He kept his spirits up with high-adrenaline hobbies, like flying tiny planes, riding motorcycles, and skydiving.

Not long after his visit to the house in Phillipsville, Bob heard that Steven, the sixty-four-year-old homeowner, had been arrested. His wizard-like mug shot even made the front page of the local paper. It turned out that a concealed trap door in the house led to a basement where, under blazing lights, Steven and a couple of partners grew more than 3,300 marijuana plants, most of which were tiny clones.

Bob wasn't even that surprised when he heard the news. He figured the guy would get off on probation. It just seemed to Bob like everyone got off on probation these days. To him, there was just no accountability and no incentive not to grow pot in Humboldt County. The district attorney, Paul Gallegos, had even attended a fund-raiser sponsored by the Humboldt Growers Association. If that wasn't condoning pot growing, Bob didn't know what was. He felt like he was pointlessly fighting the tide. The way he saw it, as long as there was a black market somewhere, the issues of criminality associated with the marijuana industry would continue. The only way it was ever going to change was to legalize it. The laws were already in place, he figured; just treat it like alcohol. You aren't allowed to come to work drunk, so you aren't allowed to come to work stoned. You don't drive drunk, you don't drive stoned. Legalize pot, tax it, and enforce laws pertaining to it. To Bob, it seemed like the only answer.

CHAPTER FIFTEEN

The Vote

O n the night of November 2, 2010, Mare Abidon loaded up her small woodstove so that it would burn low and steady through the night, and curled up in the tangle of pillows, blankets, and stuffed animals that covered her bed. As Lucky settled into his usual spot at her feet, Mare reached over and switched on the radio, and the sound of the community radio station KMUD-FM filled the cabin.

Broadcasting out of a beige one-story house surrounded by apple trees in downtown Redway, KMUD had been the voice and soundtrack of the Southern Humboldt community ever since it first crackled onto the airwaves in 1987. Its regular programming included a weekly talk show called *Thank Jah It's Friday*, the syndicated news program *Democracy Now!*, and a monthly astrology-themed cosmic weather report. The station's music shows ranged from folk and blues to salsa and world beats. Some of KMUD's more down-home touches included seemingly endless notices about lost-and-found pit bulls and pledge drive thank-you gifts of free-range eggs from local chickens.

Like the listeners who supported it, KMUD also had a rebellious side. The station broadcasted warnings about the movements of CAMP and other drug agents in the area. A few months before Election Night, for instance, a female announcer interrupted regular programming with this emergency update: "According to a citizen's observation, at eight forty-five a.m., three helicopters were seen heading from Laytonville to Bell Springs Road."

It had long been community tradition to phone KMUD, or a local organization called the Civil Liberties Monitoring Project, to report sightings of, say, a ten-vehicle convoy near Whitethorn, or a helicopter with nets full of confiscated marijuana plants flying low near a local school. The station would then broadcast the information as a news alert so, throughout the hills, people would know where law enforcement were headed. KMUD took the "phone tree" Bob Hamilton experienced to a whole new level. When members of the Humboldt Marijuana Eradication Task Force were bouncing down some godforsaken dirt road on their way to a bust, they used to joke that if they wanted to know where they were, all they had to do was turn on KMUD.

But on the night of the vote, the focus at the tiny radio station wasn't on the actions of law enforcement in the community, but on the law itself—in particular, Proposition 19, the Regulate, Control, and Tax Cannabis Act, the measure that threatened to send tumbleweeds blowing across

Humboldt or turn the place into a destination for marijuana tourism, depending on how you looked at it.

Mare was hoping for the latter. A few weeks earlier, she'd mailed in her ballot, on which she checked the box *for* legalization. Prop 19 wasn't a perfect law, and she felt it favored the industrial, indoor growers, but it was a step forward. Judging from her neighbors, Mare knew the vote was going to be close. Half said they were voting for it and half against it. Even those closest to Mare were divided.

The difference between two of her best friends was a perfect example. Both had been members of the women's consciousness-raising group with Mare back in the day, and both were fellow Back-to-the-Landers and old-growth growers who had been at it since the beginning. One grew with her daughter and ran a shop in town, and she had joined the collective with Mare. The other was one of the first members of the counterculture to settle on the coast. She was a sweet, wonderful lady who was scared of legalization. Prices had already dropped so much, and she depended on marijuana money to make ends meet. The woman had children, and hoped to have grandchildren, and while she sympathized with Mare's desire to be legal, her economic security was just too important.

Mare didn't have descendants to worry about. She had a small pension from her years of teaching art that she could live off, and when it came down to it, idealism was what was most important to her. It was an ideological thing, even though, in the past seven months since her official coming-out as a pot grower, her fantasy about how wonderful life would be when pot was legal was giving way to the realization that there didn't really seem to be much place for her in the modern, rapidly changing industry. The Tea House Collective wasn't going well. It had tried to get a permit to open a dispensary in Berkeley and been denied, and sales through its online delivery service had been abysmal since its summer launch. Depending on how things went with the collective and the vote, Mare was still considering retirement.

———

One man who was doing quite well in the new, rapidly changing pot world was Richard Lee. In all the national and international news coverage leading up to the vote, Lee was mentioned in almost every article. The man most associated with Proposition 19 did not come from the counterculture. He was a soft-spoken Texan who had come to marijuana through medicine. Two decades earlier, when Lee was twenty-seven and working as a lighting technician for the band Aerosmith, he fell while setting up for a concert in New Jersey and broke his back in a way that left him paralyzed from the waist down. Marijuana, he discovered, was the only thing that seemed to soothe the muscle spasms that came with sitting in a wheelchair.

In the year following the accident, Lee was carjacked in Houston. While waiting for almost an hour for the police to show up, he decided they were probably out busting people for marijuana. "I felt like, here was this wonderful medicine of cannabis that helped me so much, and why were the cops going after people using and selling it instead of the psychos and sociopaths who are out there robbing people?" Lee would later tell the *San Francisco Chronicle*. "I thought I should do something about it."

"Something" meant becoming an advocate for the plant. Lee ran a hemp clothing store in Houston before moving to California in the late 1990s. A decade later, he opened Oaksterdam University in downtown Oakland. The nation's first marijuana trade school offered coursework in how to grow pot, manage a dispensary, start a delivery service, and understand the intricacies of marijuana law. Lee also owned a coffee shop–style dispensary nearby called Blue Sky, and a nursery that sold marijuana clones.

By all accounts, he was doing quite well under the medical marijuana model, but in 2009, he decided it was time to take things a step further. California was in crisis, and facing a $20 billion budget shortfall in the coming year; violence among drug cartels in Mexico had claimed tens of thousands of lives, and was funded in part by marijuana sales north of the border; and the national economy was continuing its decline. Lee thought the time was right to put forward a measure to legalize and tax pot outright. It seemed like a win-win situation: the state would save money by not having to enforce its marijuana laws, and cities and counties would gain tax revenue. Many other marijuana-legalization advocates thought it would be wiser to wait until 2012, when more pot-friendly youth would turn out to vote in the presidential election, but Lee pushed on, and he put his money where his mouth was. In total, he put up more than $1.4 million to collect the signatures that put Prop 19 on the ballot.

As expected, Richard Lee was not a popular man in Humboldt County.

And he knew it.

"If the narcs don't kill me, the growers will," he told a Humboldt journalist in the summer before the vote.

Lee, it seemed, had little sympathy for the mom-and-pop growers who had started the industry and who would most likely go out of business if the RAND Corporation analysis was correct and the price of pot dropped to $400 a pound after legalization—or at least that's how he came across in a story that ran on the cover of the Humboldt alt-weekly *The North Coast Journal* in July.

"It is black market prices right now," Lee said, "and there's nothing we can do to keep little mom-and-pop places going that were making the money they were making before."

The article made some growers in Humboldt think that maybe the vote was really just some kind of ploy for Lee to fatten his bank account and strengthen his hold on the industry. Already the majority of pot sold by dispensaries around the state was grown indoors. The City of Oakland had even gone so far as to approve permits for those four gigantic indoor commercial grows that everyone was calling pot factories.

The future of the Humboldt farmer seemed uncertain, but toward the end of the article, Lee offered some ideas for how they might survive in a free market.

"Well, the tourism factor," he said. "You've got beautiful redwoods, you got beautiful country up there. You have stuff to offer that we don't have."

When asked about the marijuana, the organic, sun-grown sinsemilla that Back-to-the-Landers had pioneered decades back, well, Lee had some suggestions there, too.

"The outdoor," he said. "I was thinking they'll have to start making a lot of hash out of that."

The comment was the equivalent of telling a proud vintner that they should turn their wine into sangria, or insinuating that a strawberry farmer's berries were fit only for jam.

Lee's views only fed the paranoia.

Growers in Humboldt and throughout the Emerald Triangle, those marijuana moonshiners, were worried about their place in the new legal industry for good reason.

At the end of alcohol prohibition in 1933, there were tens of thousands of illegal distilleries. Today, the American alcohol industry is dominated by a handful of multinational corporations, including Anheuser-Busch, Constellation Brands, Pernod Ricard, and Diageo. As for the more romantic, idyllic side of the business, the one that some folks in Humboldt were hoping to emulate—that Napa Valley vintner surrounded by rows of grapes with tourists knocking at his cellar door? The sad truth is that many of the valley's wineries are actually owned by those same international liquor companies, and the typical "small" Napa winery owner in 2010 was actually a retired millionaire who'd made his fortune elsewhere.

The campaigns for and against Prop 19 were both low budget and high profile, thanks to a steady stream of media attention as the rest of the nation and the world looked at California with curiosity and, in some cases, hope.

"May God let it pass," said the former Mexican president Vicente Fox. He believed that California would set an example for the rest of the nation if it legalized marijuana, and that other states would soon follow. If that happened, the profits of the drug cartels who were waging a bloody war in his country might be reduced.

Among those who came out in support of Prop 19 were billionaire philanthropist George Soros, members of the California senate, labor unions, Bay Area congresswoman Barbara Lee, a few Silicon Valley billionaires, the United Food and Commercial Workers International Union, the American Federation of Teachers, and former U.S. surgeon general Joycelyn Elders.

"What I think is horrible about all of this is that we criminalize young people," Elders told CNN. "It's a nontoxic substance."

Other groups who endorsed 19 included the National Black Police Association and the National Latino Officers Association, who supported the measure for the same reasons as the California chapters of the National Association for the Advancement of Colored People (NAACP) and the American Civil Liberties Union (ACLU). Their reasons had less to do with pot and more to do with who was getting busted for using it.

The simple truth is that those who bear the brunt of the nation's marijuana laws are not the pot growers of Humboldt County and the rest of the Emerald Triangle; nor are they the members of law enforcement, who operate in a gray area; instead, they are young blacks and Latinos, who use pot less than whites, yet are arrested at double, triple, and sometimes even quadruple the rate.

That summer of 2010, the Drug Policy Alliance published a study that illustrated this with some shocking statistics. The study focused specifically on California, but other studies have documented the same pattern in New York and other American cities and states. In Los Angeles County, for instance, the study found that blacks make up approximately 10 percent of the population yet account for 30 percent of all those arrested for marijuana possession. In San Diego County, they make up 5.6 percent of the population and account for 20 percent of all those arrested. The study also determined that, across the state, 70 to 80 percent of people arrested for marijuana possession were under thirty.

These were the young people being criminalized whom Joycelyn Elders was talking about. Marijuana arrests create a permanent drug crime record, even if they were just a misdemeanor. These records show up during background checks by employers, landlords, credit agencies, schools, and others, and ultimately affect one's chances in life.

Before the vote, Alice Huffman, the president of the California chapter of the NAACP, wrote in *The Huffington Post* that being caught up in the criminal justice system does a lot more harm to young people than using marijuana.

Opponents of Prop 19 included almost every Democrat running for state office, both state senators, and all the major gubernatorial candidates, including Jerry Brown, who'd signed the state's landmark marijuana-decriminalization law back when he was first governor in 1976, which eliminated felony charges for possession.

"We've got to compete with China, and if everybody's stoned, how the hell are we going to make it?" Brown asked.

The strange bedfellows included Dennis Peron, one of the coauthors of the state's medical marijuana law, who said he was against 19 because he viewed all pot use as medical. Mothers Against Drunk Driving feared the law would lead to an increase in drugged drivers, and the U.S. Chamber of Commerce believed employers wouldn't be able to discipline stoned workers under it. The California Beer and Beverage Distributors, a beer trade association, also contributed money to the "No on 19" campaign. And as to be expected, many lawmen came out against, including the California Police Chiefs Association, the California State Sheriffs' Association, and the California Association of Highway Patrolmen.

But there was also a group of dissenters who spoke out in favor of legalization. They called themselves Law Enforcement Against Prohibition (LEAP), and were a group of retired judges, police officers, and others who said they had experienced the War on Drugs from the front lines and saw that it wasn't working.

"I have learned that most bad things about marijuana—especially the violence made inevitable by an obscenely profitable black market—are caused by the prohibition, not the plant," retired San Jose police chief Joseph McNamara wrote in an editorial in the *San Francisco Chronicle*.

To the parents who were concerned that legalization would result in an explosion of pot use, especially among young people, McNamara pointed out that the United States had some of the world's strictest marijuana laws, and at the same time, the world's highest pot use rate, twice that of the famously liberal Netherlands. Studies indicated that marijuana use was not good for developing teenage brains, but pot prohibition didn't make it harder for kids to get their hands on it. McNamara cited a recent Columbia University study that found that teenagers said it was easier for them to buy illegal pot than government-regulated booze.

The polls bounced back and forth during the summer, and for many months, 19 was ahead. In September, according to a field poll, 49 percent of California voters favored legalization. By late October, only 44 percent polled said they intended to vote for it.

On the night of the vote, no one knew which way it would go.

Around the same time Mare was lying in her bed listening to the radio, closer to town, in a 1960s-era ranch house surrounded by a tall wooden fence, Crockett Randall was getting ready to take a shower. He peeled off his clothes and dropped them onto a linoleum floor that was covered with soggy towels. The house belonged to Frankie. It was the one where the door next to the bathroom opened into a brightly lit room where even more little money trees grew. Down the hall, in a living room decorated in a style that can only be described as bachelor-stoner, with orange walls, sarong curtains, and leather couches, Frankie and Zavie were awaiting news of 19 on a giant flat-screen TV.

Harvest was still in full swing, and while Crockett enjoyed being around female energy after all that time alone in the cabin, by this point, after spending practically twenty-four hours a day surrounded by others, he was tired of it all—of Zavie's incessant drinking, and of people complaining about the bad Mexican food at the restaurant in Phillipsville. He was ready to be done and move back home. But first he had to let the hot water wash off a day's worth of resin and sweat.

Shortly after 9:00 p.m., CNN reporter Wolf Blitzer delivered the news.

"Marijuana will not be legal in California. Not today."

Crockett was in the shower when he heard Zavie and Frankie shouting. He threw on a towel and ran dripping down the hallway.

"Did it fail?"

"Yes!" they shouted.

"Yeah!" he cheered, and then jokingly added, "Let's double the price!"

In the end, Crockett was so indifferent that he hadn't even bothered to vote, but he still felt like celebrating.

Elsewhere in Humboldt, other whoops and cheers filled the air.

Inside the Brass Rail, a former bordello for loggers that was now a combination steakhouse and Thai restaurant, this affirmation was heard in the bar above the jubilant cries that followed news of the measure's defeat:

"We won't be a ghost town!"

In her cabin out at the coast, Mare sighed.

After all those years, it had seemed that legalization might finally happen.

But it wasn't to be. The jails weren't yet going to be emptied of the people arrested for marijuana. She and her friends weren't yet going to be able to claim their roles as master growers. And the pot bushes around her deck would also have to wait.

Mare shut off the radio in disappointment.

Then, because her personality was one that always looks for the bright side, she realized it wasn't the end of the world. It just meant not yet. In one way or another, she thought, marijuana legalization is definitely on the way. Maybe the next time it appeared on the ballot it wouldn't seem to favor the industrial grower so much. Mare shut her eyes and began to drift off to sleep, Lucky snored, and the wood in the stove at the end of her bed burned warm and low.

———

Two hundred miles away, in the living room of a sage-green house in the town of Chico, Emma Worldpeace cracked open her laptop to have a look at the news. She'd just finished a day at the bike shop, and eaten dinner with Ethan. Over the past few weeks, while coming and going from work, Emma had noticed a group of young people campaigning for Prop 19 in front of the Safeway grocery store next door. Emma thought it was great that they were getting out there informing people about legalization. She had voted for 19 via absentee ballot in Humboldt. She knew it was going to be a close vote but couldn't help but feel bummed when she read the results.

"Prop 19 didn't pass," she told Ethan.

It felt like a step backward to Emma. Here California was the first state to authorize medical marijuana, and now Californians had chosen to continue to waste money locking people up for growing and using marijuana, and to reject what Emma saw as an opportunity to bring in tax revenues for schools. Emma just didn't get it.

———

Early the next morning, in a house in Shelter Cove that looked out over the Pacific Ocean, Bob Hamilton turned on his computer and scanned the news. Bob never stayed up for election results, not even presidential ones. Like everyone else in Humboldt, he wasn't as interested in the Republican sweep of the House or that Jerry Brown had been elected governor again.

Bob had voted for legalization, and couldn't help but feel disappointment when he read that 19 had lost, though he wasn't that surprised.

He figured the majority of Californians still didn't approve of marijuana. He also reckoned that all the people making money from it wanted their profits to stay high. A few weeks earlier, he had peeled some "Save Humboldt County, Keep Pot Illegal" stickers off a mailbox at the Whitethorn Post Office. These were the same stickers Frankie had stuck up in his house near Garberville. They gave Bob a good laugh, but he didn't leave them on the mailbox, because they were vandalizing federal property. He figured that no one who grew or sold pot wanted 19 to pass.

But he wasn't exactly right.

In the end, all three pot-producing counties of the Emerald Triangle rejected legalization. The numbers in Humboldt were 46.8 percent in favor, 53.2 percent opposed, which closely mirrored the statewide results; the measure failed in California 46.5 to 53.5. In SoHum, the numbers against legalization were even higher: 65.6 percent against and 34.4 percent for.

The irony that the majority of voters in California's pot-producing heartland were against legalization wasn't lost in the news cycle, and some of the comments following the news coverage were not kind.

"Let's grab machetes and head up to Humboldt...

Humboldt, your little community just pissed off a ton of people who are sick of paying your inflated crop prices!" read one comment on a *Huffington Post* story.

Another commenter on an article on the *Mother Jones* website: "I would encourage all in California to boycott weed grown in the Triangle, the citizens of which voted overwhelmingly against Prop 19 to protect their own profits. Let them choke on their own smoke."

But in the end, the reasons the measure failed weren't because of pot growers. Residents of the Emerald Triangle represent just a sliver of the state's population. The midterm elections saw a lower turnout among marijuana-friendly youth voters. In an off-year election cycle, people who turn out to vote are often older and more conservative. Midterm elections are not traditionally the time when progressive initiatives are passed, especially one as underfunded as Prop 19. Two other things had happened that fall that might also have helped sway the vote.

In late September, Governor Arnold Schwarzenegger, who opposed Prop 19, signed a bill into law that reduced the penalty for possession of less than an ounce of pot from a misdemeanor to an infraction, which was the equivalent of a parking ticket and meant that one could get off with a $100 fine and no criminal record. This helped enforce the idea that pot was pretty much already as good as legal in California. The new law, however, did nothing to address the sale, transportation, or cultivation of the drug, which of course remained entirely illegal on a federal level.

Then, in October, a few weeks before the vote, U.S. attorney general Eric Holder threatened a showdown with Washington if California legalized pot outright. In a letter, Holder vowed to fight Prop 19 and "vigorously enforce" federal drug laws.

And so Prop 19 failed. If there was a silver lining to it all, it was that Prop 19 pushed marijuana legalization into mainstream American politics, and helped pave the way for two successful legalization initiatives in other states two years later.

After reading the news that morning, Bob Hamilton finished his coffee and caught one last glimpse of the ocean before he headed out the door and began the drive back to a job that would continue exactly as it had the day before, in that frustrating place known as the gray area.

CHAPTER SIXTEEN

Bob

In the year following the vote, Bob Hamilton chased convicts, chopped down illegal gardens, encouraged transients to move on, and got lost on dirt roads searching for fake addresses listed on arrest warrants. But he did it all with a different attitude. In this community of secrets, he now had one of his own.

Around the time of the vote, Bob and his wife met with their accountant. She handed them a folder, and when they opened it, they found a piece of paper inside that read, "Congratulations! You can retire at 50!" It turned out that those years of working hard and saving and making safe investments looked like they were going to pay off for the Hamiltons. Though Bob was more than ready for a change, he and his wife decided to be prudent and wait to retire until their daughter Jessica was out of college and settled in a job. But they set a date, and in July 2013, Bob Hamilton would turn in his badge, and he and his wife would begin a new life somewhere else. They would leave the futility of his fight behind.

That was more than two years out, and unfortunately, knowing his departure date gave Bob quite a case of short-timer's disease, one that made putting up with the "pot shit" even harder. In the spring, when Dazey's Supply was having its annual sale, complete with a reggae concert, free veggie burgers, and vendors selling everything needed to grow a healthy pot garden, Bob drove by and just shook his head. It looked like a fair for dope growers. Another time, Bob let out a yelp when he caught Solar Dan, an old hippie who rides an electric skateboard, sparking up in front of Redwood Realty in Garberville, right next to a No Loitering sign. Solar Dan had a thick German accent and a bead that hung from his beard like a tassel. His nickname came from his fondness for lighting his joints with a magnifying glass and the sun. He had recently begun holding meetings about the idea of renaming Garberville and Redway the "Emerald City," because he thought it would help locals take charge of their "ganja future."

"I'm not loitering, I'm waiting," Solar Dan told Bob dismissively, as he exhaled a fragrant cloud of pot smoke into the air.

In the end, the short-timer's disease may have affected Bob's attitude, but it didn't affect his job performance. He still had two of the sharpest eyes in Southern Humboldt, and maybe the sharpest nose, which turned out to be very unfortunate for one particular pot smuggler.

In November 2011, almost exactly a year after the vote,

Bob Hamilton pulled through the parking lot of the Best Western Inn in Garberville on his way to the sheriff's substation next door. Out of the corner of his eye he spied a Chevy Suburban that was parked a little funny. It had a cargo trailer attached and Michigan plates and was taking up multiple parking spaces. Deep in the back of his mind, Bob thought, Bet that guy's hauling dope. Then the thought passed, and Bob arrived at the station and filled out his report.

A little while later, Bob pulled back out and onto Conger Street when that same Suburban passed right in front of him, and the powerful scent of what smelled like an entire family of skunks curled out the vents of the trailer and right up Bob's nose. The guy was hauling dope, all right, poorly packaged, smelly dope.

Bob pulled the Suburban over just before Alderpoint Road.

The driver was a white man in his thirties. He was clean cut and seemed a little nervous.

Bob told him why he'd stopped him.

"I think you're transporting. I smelled a big odor of marijuana coming out of this trailer," he said. "We can handle this two ways. I can call and get a search warrant, or you can be cooperative."

"Am I still going to go to jail?" the driver asked.

"Oh, yes," Bob replied. "But it'll be in your favor in the report."

When he opened the trailer, Bob found that it was filled with ninety-two cardboard boxes. Inside the boxes were more than 275 pounds of pot. It was the biggest traffic stop bust of his career. (Bob's previous transportation bust record was 80 pounds.) He also found $10,000 in cash and $2,000 in money orders. The marijuana was surely destined for out of state, which would have been a federal felony. Bob figured that since it was Humboldt County, the driver would probably get off on probation.

A few weeks later, Bob had one of those days when he helped protect the grower from the outside man.

When he arrived at work early that November morning, he learned that a home invasion had just taken place in Benbow, a community of some three hundred people situated around a golf course, just south of Garberville. Just before four o'clock that morning, a forty-one-year-old man was asleep in his bed with his twenty-one-year-old wife and their small child when the man was awoken by a strange noise. When he got up to investigate, he found an intruder standing in his hallway. The intruder was wearing a mask that was pulled down tight over his face and was pointing a gun at him.

"Give me your fucking money and I'll leave," the intruder said.

Behind the intruder, the homeowner saw the shadowy outline of another uninvited guest. This wasn't good. The homeowner produced $1,000 in cash.

"I need more money than that. Give me everything you got!" the intruder screamed.

Then he pointed his gun at the homeowner and pulled the trigger. The bullet grazed the top of the man's skull but didn't pierce it. The wound was bleeding, as head wounds do, but he was alive. The intruder told him that he would kill him if he didn't come up with more cash.

The man handed over another $3,000 and his wife's wedding ring. The two suspects then fled.

In a study conducted the following year, the Humboldt County Sheriff's Department determined that twenty-eight home invasions were reported in the county over the eight-year period from 2003 to 2011. All the invasions took place in homes where marijuana was grown, bought, or sold. In many of the cases, people were shot or stabbed. The sheriff, Michael Downey, suspected that the actual number of violent robberies was much higher. Downey figured that there were many cases where growers survived such incidents— battered and bruised maybe, but in one piece—and didn't report them. After all, how do you report that someone stole your contraband, or the large amount of cash you just happened to have lying around?

In this case, the injured man and his wife called the sheriff.

After Bob arrived at work early that morning, he was instructed to stake out a red Volvo that was parked near the house. In what was clearly not the best-planned rip-off in history, the robbers appeared to have left behind a getaway car. They didn't come back for it, but by tracking the car's owner, the Sheriff's Department learned that a suspect in the robbery might be staying at a local hotel. He was described as having short-cut black hair, a beard, and being of Middle Eastern descent.

A little while later, a man matching that description cracked open the door and stepped out of a room at the Garberville Motel, another one of the town's run-down one-star lodging options. Bob was waiting in his vehicle nearby, and the moment he saw the man, he entered a heightened state of nerves and awareness. Whoever had ripped off that man in Benbow earlier that morning had a gun and wasn't afraid to use it. In a rush of adrenaline, Bob shot his car across the parking lot toward his suspect, who had just popped open the trunk of a white sedan. Bob screeched to a stop in front of the sedan and ordered the man and the people sitting in the car to put their hands up. In the car's trunk, Bob found a bag filled with damp dark clothing and two gray knit stocking caps with eyeholes cut out of them.

The suspect was a twenty-five-year-old Yemeni American from Oakland named Hussain Obad. When Bob searched Obad's pockets after he'd handcuffed him, he found $1,634 and the keys to the red Volvo.

While Bob guided Obad into his vehicle, the young man looked up at him and asked, in a matter-of-fact manner, "So, boss, how many years do you think I'll get?"

The truth was, Bob didn't know.

———

Two months later, in January 2012, Bob Hamilton found himself zipping along the highway between Eureka and Arcata, past the massive warehouses of the California Redwood Company and the row of eucalyptus trees that stand like guardians along Humboldt Bay. He was on his way to work.

Bob had been reassigned. Due to the state's financial crisis, fourteen positions in the Humboldt Sheriff's Department had been frozen and another five people had left. This meant that services to rural areas such as SoHum were reduced, and Bob was moved to cover a bedroom community north of the city of Arcata called McKinleyville.

That same year, budget cuts caused the state of California to "leave the drug trade," in the words of Sheriff Michael Downey. In 2012, the enemy of the marijuana grower known as CAMP was restructured and renamed. In its first year, the Cannabis Eradication and Reclamation Team (CERT) operated for four days in the county, compared to what used to be eight weeks of CAMP.

Initially, Bob was bummed when he got word of his transfer. He thought Northern Humboldt would be full of "tweakers," or meth users, but the assignment ended up being a welcome change of pace. There were fewer transients and zero hippie buses broken down alongside the road. Sure, there were still pockets of what Bob called "junkyard mentality"—front yards decorated with burnt-out cars and bleak trailer parks that were home to people hanging on by a very frayed thread—but there seemed less of it than there was down south. Then there was the wonderful fact that roads Bob now rolled on were all paved, which meant he could get everywhere he needed to go so much quicker. He did not miss rumbling up dusty or muddy track with the sound of a banjo playing in the back of his mind. The other silver lining was that Bob wasn't sent to the courts. That, he figured, would have been so damn boring it would have made him want to eat his gun.

When Bob left the Garberville substation, that building he hated, and feared contained asbestos, he left his mark on the Missing and Wanted person's wall near the secretary's desk. Next to the Missing flyer for Robert Firestone, the old man with dementia who had gone walking and was never seen again, Bob stuck one of those amusing "Save Humboldt County, Keep Pot Illegal" stickers he'd peeled off a mailbox before the vote. Above the Wanted poster for Keith Conn, the "real bad motherfucker" whom Bob never managed to catch, he taped an article from the local paper about how the Humboldt Growers Association had hosted a fund-raiser for the district attorney's reelection campaign that past fall. The part about how the growers had raised $5,000 for the D.A. was marked in yellow highlighter.

To Bob, that said it all.

———

Northern Humboldt proved to be a different world. Of course pot was grown there, and "unemployed" boys drove big expensive trucks—it was still Humboldt after all—but it was nothing at the level it was down south. The foggy coastal climate meant that a lot of people grew indoors, which made it all seem much more discreet.

On some days up north, when Bob was between calls from, say, a trailer park manager who wanted to evict a tenant and a woman whose bedroom had been trashed by an ex-boyfriend, he would catch fleeting glimpses of the raw beauty he adored. While on a drive through Prairie Creek Redwoods State Park, he'd marvel at the Roosevelt elk, with their antlers that looked like the forked branches of an oak tree. On the way back to the highway, he'd take in the moss-covered trees that lined the road through the park. They were so fuzzy and surreal they seemed straight out of the pages of Dr. Seuss.

Humboldt County was a beautiful place, there was no mistaking it, but it had become like a Hollywood set for Bob. It was like a façade, and behind the façade was a different story, one of trash, and meth, and familial dysfunction. Of course it wasn't just Humboldt. Cops deal with the margins and extremes of society everywhere; the bowels, as Bob put it. His pessimism about the place was an occupational hazard, and he knew it. Sometimes he wished he had never returned to Humboldt, had never gotten to know its underbelly and learn what lurked behind the trees. It could have stayed a place of perfect beauty for him, like the way he saw it when he was a kid.

But there was no going back, and maybe that was the lesson. There was only going forward, and Bob had a date to move toward: July 2013.

He and his wife were busy working on the plan. They had spent a few weeks that past September in Italy. They flew into Rome and drove out into the countryside, where they spent ten days participating in the grape harvest in Le Marche. Then they pushed on to Tuscany, where they ate cheese and cold cuts and drank wine, and met a man who might be interested in having them help run his B&B. That was the dream, a B&B or maybe an olive grove somewhere in Italy for part of the year. The other half of their time, the Hamiltons were considering working as volunteers for international disaster relief with the Red Cross. Bob would be former law enforcement, and his wife was a nurse; these were skills sure to come in handy somewhere.

Helping people was ingrained in Bob, and he wanted to do it in a way that was productive and felt good. People loved firefighters, but not everyone loved cops. Volunteering in emergency situations sounded like a way in which Bob could use his skills and people might actually appreciate him.

In the meantime, he had a job to finish and a deadline to shoot for.

"Only five months, twenty days, and eight hours to go," he'd say at the start of a workday, and then he'd laugh. "But who's counting?"

CHAPTER SEVENTEEN

Emma

One March evening in 2011, when the rain fell in steady sheets, Emma Worldpeace slid an apple crisp into the oven at her home in Chico. Ethan sat at the desk in the living room, where the bluegrass music of Gillian Welch played on the stereo. Emma pecked her boyfriend on the cheek and then bent over him to quickly check her e-mail. A message from the Chico State University admissions office awaited in her in-box. A couple of months earlier, Emma had applied to the school's master's of social work program. In her application, she wrote that she saw social workers as agents of change who worked to create peaceful communities.

"I can see myself thriving as a high school counselor, a youth caseworker, or a program facilitator," Emma wrote. "I would love to return and practice social work in a rural community, like the one where I grew up in southern Humboldt County, or another part of Northern California."

In the bio section of the application, Emma wrote about her past with her typical unflinching honesty.

"My childhood was anything but idyllic. My father was a stubborn alcoholic, in and out of jail and absent for most of my foundational years. My mother struggled to raise six children on her own, relying on meager welfare checks and the illegal cultivation of marijuana to keep the rent paid and put food on the table," she wrote.

"I benefited greatly from the care and attention of my teachers and other caring adults who encouraged me to apply to college, connected me with services, and acknowledged my hardships without making me feel alienated; skills I have employed myself when working with the disadvantaged."

The Chico State School of Social Work apparently liked what they read.

"Hey, I got in!" she told Ethan. "They just sent the message."

"Sweet!" said Ethan, as he brought his hand down playfully on her butt.

"Emma's going to grad school. You can be the breadwinner, and I'll retire."

"Yeah, I'm going to be rolling in it as a social worker," she said, laughing.

———

Over the course of the following year, Emma returned to Humboldt for Mother's Day, the annual Summer Arts and

Music Festival, and to participate in a hundred-mile bike ride along the coast. In September, around the time Emma started back to school, Mike's preliminary hearing was held in Eureka, and was covered by the press. It was the first anyone had heard from the men who were in the garden that day. Emma read the news coverage when she returned home in the evening. The testimonies were quite vivid. One of the men whom Mike allegedly shot, a Guatemalan named Fernando Lopez, described the events leading up to the shooting, how their work plans had changed and they wanted to leave, and how Mike had shown up and started shooting. Lopez had a scar the size of a nickel in his right cheek, from where the bullet entered him. He described how he and his friend Mario Roberto Juarez-Madrid ran for the woods after the shots were fired, and how he heard his friend scream and fall, and then pick himself up and continue running. It was the last time Lopez ever saw his friend.

"He was a good man," Lopez said in Spanish, through an interpreter. Then he broke down crying. The good man left behind a wife and two children back in Guatemala. A Sheriff's Department detective testified during the hearing that Juarez-Madrid had been shot in the back, and then in the head at point-blank range.

Lopez spent the night on the run in the woods while Mike hunted him, Lopez said, by the light of the full moon. He prayed for his survival to the tiny Virgin Mary figurine he carried in his hand. Lopez's story then took on elements of myth. Sometime during the night, he said, he stumbled upon a group of eight bears and threw rocks at them so they wouldn't approach him. Just after dawn, he reached the California Department of Forestry and Fire Protection base in Kneeland, where firefighters are housed during the wildfire season. There, Lopez collapsed on the ground and called for help.

Emma read the stories filled with both sadness and horror. So much of what she read sounded so earnest. One part that didn't sit well with her, though, was the part about the eight bears, since she didn't really know them to travel in packs. She also wondered who the hell the other people were who were mentioned in the news coverage. Who was this guy named Tom Tuohy, who seemed to have connected Mike with the workers? Would this Tuohy character be charged with human trafficking?

Emma felt really hopeless about the situation. At this point, she thought if Mike were found guilty, it looked like he would be spending his life in prison, which was really sad.

As much as she cared about Mike as a person, Emma hoped the legal system would work as it was supposed to and that if Mike had committed the crimes he was accused of, he would be brought to justice and would serve time.

Mike's trial was set to begin in early 2012. The Humboldt County D.A., Paul Gallegos, had dropped the marijuana cultivation charges to focus on the murder and attempted murder charges, for which Mike faced twenty-five years to life.

Meanwhile, Emma was busy with her classes and internship. At the same time, her mother, Sage, had finally separated from Mike's father, Jim, and was in the process of buying a house when she went through a very public mental health breakdown. Sage was in and out of Sempervirens, the county psychiatric health facility. Emma was so preoccupied with her mother that she didn't hear anything else about Mike until early March, when her sister Aia told her over the phone that the Feds had taken over Mike's case. Emma didn't really understand the ramifications of this until she Googled it after she hung up the phone. Under federal law, Mike now potentially faced the death penalty.

Emma was shocked. She was against the death penalty in general. She thought it was a big waste of money to keep people on death row. Maybe, she thought, it should be reserved for the worst of the worst, people with a long history of violent crime, but that isn't Mike. Later, after Emma had spoken to more people about the case and given it some more thought, it made sense that the Feds had gotten involved. She figured that Mike's case would be used as fodder in the larger political conversation taking place about marijuana legalization in the state and beyond. On one hand, there were the pro-marijuana people, who say it's harmless and point out that people don't die from smoking it; and then you have the people who think marijuana is a dangerous drug, and that bad things happen because of it. The shooting was marijuana-related violence. Emma figured the Feds would take Mike's case and hold it up and say, "Look at how horrible these violent pot growers are." "Here was this big-time grower with pit bulls who hired undocumented immigrants," they could say, "and then this heartless monster couldn't afford to pay them, so he allegedly shot them, and then he allegedly hunted them through the night to try to make sure they were dead." Emma figured the Feds would use Mike's case as an example of why marijuana is bad and why we needed to keep investing money in arresting people and locking them up for growing and using it.

A couple of weeks later, in an interview with the Bay Area radio station KQED, Melinda Haag, the U.S. attorney for California's Northern District, referred to Mike's case in that very way.

"We indicted a case two weeks ago in Humboldt County. There's a grower there who allegedly had a fifteen-hundred-plant grow operation. He allegedly hired undocumented workers from Central America, and the indictment alleges that when those workers came to him and asked to be paid, he instead pulled out a gun, shot and killed one of them, and chased the other one through the woods, shooting," Haag said.

"I believe there's this notion out there that the marijuana industry is just full of organic farmers who are peacefully growing an organic, natural plant and that there's no harm associated with that. And what I hear from people in the community is that there is harm."

The focus of the interview was on a larger issue of a series of actions Haag and three other California U.S. attorneys had recently taken to try to rein in the state's medical marijuana industry. The press dubbed it the "Cannabis Crackdown." It angered people who saw it as a move by the Obama administration to backtrack on a promise to respect states' rights when it comes to medical marijuana. As part of the crackdown, letters were sent to dispensaries around the state threatening their landlords with property seizure if they didn't shut their doors. Hundreds closed. On April 2, 2012, one hundred DEA agents raided Oaksterdam University, while an angry crowd of protestors outside chanted, "DEA, go away!" and "Go after real criminals!" Afterward, under what could only have been a serious threat, Richard Lee, the school's founder and the man who had bankrolled Prop 19, relinquished ownership of his school. Another symbolic federal raid occurred a few months earlier, when the DEA busted a high-profile Mendocino County medical pot grower named Matthew Cohen. If there was a teacher's pet among pot growers, it was Cohen. He was one of the most law-abiding growers around. Cohen registered his plants with the Sheriff's Office for a fee; he even taxed his trimmers. He lived in an area filled with illegal grows, but by raiding him and chopping down his plants, the Feds sent a clear message to lawmakers attempting to regulate the industry and to anyone trying to work within the state law, that they didn't consider any of it legal and could crack down on anyone at any time.

On a sunny day in October, Emma Worldpeace stood outside the Glenn E. Dyer Detention Facility in downtown Oakland and stared up at the hulking concrete building. Somewhere inside sat Mike, and after all this time, Emma was finally going to see him. She had tried once before, on the Thanksgiving just after the shooting. Mike was still in the Humboldt County jail then, but he had already had a visitor that day, so Emma wasn't allowed in. Then, somehow, with school, work, and life, two years passed.

Once inside, Emma signed in and then took a seat in the busy visitors' waiting area. She scanned the room and realized that she was the only white person. Most of the others were Latino families, mothers and beautiful children whom they had dressed up like dolls. Emma smiled at a little girl across from her and practiced her basic Spanish while she waited for her name to be called. Then she passed through metal detectors and locked doors, and rode an elevator that reeked of cheap perfume and floor cleaner, until she reached the visiting area.

The windowless room was cold and bleak. The inmates sat in a long line behind thick glass, just like in the movies. There were little cubby-type partitions between them to give the illusion of privacy. Since Emma didn't know where Mike was, she had to walk down the entire row, peering into each cubby and making uncomfortable eye contact with the stranger sitting on the other side. A man at the very end of the row with slicked-back hair and a moustache called out her name.

When he beamed at her, she realized it was Mike.

She pulled up a chair and sat down.

"I almost didn't recognize you," she told him. The hair and moustache made him look a bit like a Latino gangster. He just laughed and then asked what she was doing in town.

Emma and Ethan had come to see a concert and were staying nearby.

"How are you doing?" she asked.

Over the course of the next forty minutes, Emma and Mike began to catch up, all the while avoiding the reason they were talking to each other through glass. In March, Mike had pled not guilty to the charges against him, but he wasn't allowed to discuss the case.

One of the first things Emma noticed about Mike, besides his new look, was that his skin was so pale he looked almost gray. It turned out that he was considered a violent, high-security-level inmate and was kept in isolation in his own cell. He was separated from other inmates by thick concrete walls, not bars. There were no cracks for Mike to whisper through when he felt starved for human contact. He was allowed into the common area for only forty-five minutes to an hour every day, and into the exercise area just once a week. The exercise area wasn't even outside, hence the sun-starved pallor.

The visiting area was full of people struggling to make themselves heard through thick plate glass, and Emma had a hard time hearing Mike above the din. Particularly after a woman a few seats down started yelling at a prisoner who appeared to be her boyfriend.

"Can you hear me?" Emma asked Mike.

He told her he could hear her just fine, and that sensory deprivation worked wonders.

They both smiled. Emma took it as a good sign that he was able to crack a joke. Mike asked about their brothers and sisters. Emma told him about her master's program, and Mike told her how much he admired her for still being in school. He remembered all of those years she studied hard at Berkeley. He had recently been working through some educational packets the jail provided, and found them really challenging. He told Emma that when he thought of her, he felt inspired to keep studying.

He also told her that he had seen her dad: EZ Out had spent a weekend in the Humboldt jail while Mike was there.

"Oh, my dad," Emma said, and started to feel embarrassed. She didn't know why he had gone to jail.

Mike reassured her that it was good to see her dad. It was as though someone he knew had shown up on his desert island. Mike said that he and EZ had spent the weekend playing cards and cribbage together.

Mike had been reading a lot. He was currently engrossed in a book on abnormal psychology and was working through the educational packets. Like many prisoners, he helped pass some of the endless downtime working out in his room. He also told Emma that he had been trying to meditate.

When it was time for her to go, Mike told her that he'd love to see the other siblings, too. Emma promised to send some photos, and to write.

Back in the fresh air and bright sunlight outside, Emma felt a little dizzy and sat down for a moment to collect her thoughts and await Ethan, who was coming to pick her up. She took some deep breaths and worried that she might break down and cry, but as she sat there, and the rays of the autumn sun warmed her face, she realized that she felt oddly reassured. Mike appeared somewhat healthy, and he seemed to be using his time to reflect. The hardest part of the whole visit, she realized, not taking into account Mike's uncertain future, was that she couldn't hug him. He looked so much like he could use a comforting hand placed gently on his shoulder.

Ethan pulled up a few minutes later.

"How was it?" he asked, as she climbed in the passenger seat, shut the door, and fastened her seat belt.

"You know what?" Emma said, as she turned and looked at him. "It was really, really good."

She still loved Mike and considered him her brother, after all, and wanted to do what she could to help him and be there for him.

CHAPTER EIGHTEEN

Crockett

U nder a waning August sun, Crockett stood outside his house in Marin County and peeled off a yellow reflective vest. He was wearing jeans, work boots, and a layer of dirt so thick it would turn his bathtub brown. He'd spent the day on a bulldozer scooping heaps of dirt out of the ground to build a pond. Crockett called the work eating dirt, because clouds of it would billow up as he worked and settle on his skin, float up his nose, invade his ears, and leave a gritty taste in his mouth. He had spent the past week running heavy equipment for the construction company he used to work for before he moved to Humboldt. He liked to play with big machines, like a boy with Tonka trucks, and the pay was decent and much needed. One of the best parts of his day was the strong, hot shower that came at the end of it, but that would have to wait. A call had just come in. His connection was ready to move some weed, and Crockett had to be in San Francisco, with the product, in less than an hour.

Crockett paused just long enough to run into his house, an old Western-style building that looked like it should have horses hitched out front. After taking a quick bong hit, he started up his Mitsubishi. Its unrestricted muffler rumbled to life like some kind of animal that needed to be put out of its misery. With Wyclef Jean playing on his stereo, and the radar detector he had bought at the Security Store in Humboldt firmly in place on his windshield, he pulled out onto the road. Almost all the hats Crockett wore were strewn around the car. On the seat next to him was his volunteer fire department radio. In the back, the reflective vest he wore while running excavators and bulldozers was resting on his backpack; and in the trunk, inside one of his smell-proof Watershed bags, were ten pounds of weed he had picked up a few minutes earlier from a friend's house nearby. All that was missing was a bag of fish emulsion or some plant stakes to represent the pot grower, but Crockett wasn't doing that this year.

Passing through town took all of fifteen seconds. There were a handful of homes, a post office, a general store, the firehouse, and the town bar, where Crockett's ex-girlfriend, the one he'd lived with for eight years, brought her new boyfriend after she and Crockett broke up, making Crockett miserable. Just outside of town, the hillside was covered with a spiny shrub with yellow flowers called gorse. It looked pretty from a distance, but up close, its thorns were thick and sharp. When Crockett was a teenager, he planted pot deep in those bushes. The thorns kept out deer, and prying eyes, and ripped Crockett's clothes to shreds. Later, more brazenly, he and his best friend grew some plants in the ditch alongside the road near the cemetery.

The pot in Crockett's trunk was grown in a greenhouse, with light deprivation, which meant it had been tricked into flowering earlier. It was a month before the start of the outdoor harvest season, and the black market would soon be flooded. Crockett's connection promised a good price: $2,400 a pound. Crockett figured whoever was buying it would probably pass it off as indoor weed back in New York City, or some other place back east where it would fetch around $4,000 a pound.

Crockett's trip to the city was a speedy example of how most California marijuana was moved around the state and across the country: as contraband in the trunks of cars. For every trailer that was intercepted by someone like Bob Hamilton, many, many more loads of pot slipped by unnoticed in car trunks, motor homes, false-bottom pickup truck beds, FedEx packages, and otherwise. Like the roots of the plant itself, marijuana distribution pipelines spread out in every direction. That was how the black market worked. It was unorganized crime.

For his three-hour effort, Crockett planned to shave $2,000 off the top. Not a bad wage for what was essentially a delivery service. All he had to do was make it there on time and avoid being caught.

The Mitsubishi was soon racing at around eighty miles an hour down a winding country road, past straw-colored hills and ramshackle barns that were skeletons of the area's once-thriving dairy and sheep ranching industries. Some of the old ranch homes had bales of fresh-cut hay piled out-side like giant yellow bricks.

A truck pulling a boat that was going less than the speed limit forced Crockett to slow down and hang back for a moment. Normally he would have passed the truck around the last corner, but because of what was in his trunk, he had to behave. In Humboldt, there was even a saying about it: one crime at a time. In other words, don't commit a misdemeanor while committing a felony. His patience lasted only a few minutes, though, and soon he was gunning his engine, guiding the Mitsubishi across the double yellow line, and rocketing past the truck and boat.

He was late.

Crockett didn't return to Humboldt that spring. After the vote, at the end of harvest, he returned home, to Marin County. Then he took off on a tropical vacation. First he went to Thailand, where he spent the majority of his time at a clinic in Bangkok having some major dental work done for the princely sum of $300. Then he joined some friends on a surfing trip to Oahu.

Frankie had wanted him to return to Humboldt and work another season, but Crockett couldn't commit. He had missed his friends too much while he was away in Humboldt, and his comfort zone. He had felt stuck in that cabin, and had lost some of his pot-dealing connections while he was living there.

Then there was the small matter that Frankie still owed him $30,000 for work he'd done that harvest.

When Crockett had first arrived in Humboldt, the deal was that he would be paid around $100,000. Then Zavie was hired on, and the amount changed. Frankie and Crockett agreed on $50,000. Frankie paid him that, but Crockett was still waiting on $30,000 for transporting the product south. Crockett had made more round trips from Humboldt to the Bay Area with his trunk full of weed than he cared to remember. In the end, after the mold and the trimming, what could have been a $1 million garden ended up being worth around half that. They pulled in about three hundred pounds. The highest they were paid per pound was $3,700. The lowest was $1,600. Then Frankie lost some money in a festival he had invested in, and Crockett had to wait on the rest of his pay.

Without work contracts, and with conditions and rates that changed in an instant, it was easy to understand how most of the violence related to marijuana was business related.

Crockett, however, did not tuck his gun into his waistband and storm off to see Frankie. He was surprisingly calm about it. When friends asked him why he wasn't angry, he'd tell them that he and Frankie grew up together and he trusted him. Crockett figured that what was coming to him was like money in the bank. Frankie had built four additional greenhouses, and was growing more pot than ever. Crockett figured he'd get a cut of the coming harvest, without having to be alone in the woods.

Marijuana debt was also part of the business. Crockett knew that. He still could have used the money, though. He had been so broke over the past few months, before he landed the temporary construction job, that he struggled to make rent. He didn't grow any pot this year, not for any reason other than that he just felt lazy and didn't have the drive.

The last time he went to Humboldt to pick up some money, things didn't go so well. Before he left, Crockett got a call on his fire department emergency radio about a man experiencing chest pains. The man, it turned out, was the owner of the local coffee shop who made Crockett's mocha every morning. He was driving home with his two-year-old child in the backseat when the chest pains started. He pulled over to call to alert his wife about what was happening. By the time Crockett arrived on the scene a few minutes later, the man's feet were swelling and he was turning blue. Crockett pulled him out of the car and did CPR on him, but the coffee shop owner was dead.

Afterward, Crockett made the three-plus-hour drive north to Humboldt to get paid. When he got there, Frankie and Zavie were high on Valium and coke, and they didn't have his money. Crockett crashed out on the leather couch in the living room, but the guys were up till 3:00 a.m. making so much noise that it was impossible to sleep.

"Fuck, you guys are assholes," Crockett told them.

Then he got back in his car and made the long drive home in inky black silence.

It was probably a good thing he didn't return to Humboldt to work with those two for months on end.

———

Crockett passed by Sausalito and was fast approaching the Golden Gate Bridge when his cell phone rang. It was his connection.

"Running late, hitting traffic," Crockett told him, as he eased to a crawl. Only two lanes were funneling traffic into the city; the rest were full of commuters heading home to Marin, Sonoma, and the rest of the North Bay.

"All good as long as you're here by seven," replied the voice on speakerphone, which belonged to a man who moved so much pot that Crockett had seen millions of dollars in cash stacked up at the guy's house. The man was tall and kind of dorky looking, not at all what you'd expect an interstate drug trafficker to look like.

But that was the marijuana industry: things were never what they seemed.

In another example of pot debt, this nerdy high-roller once owed Crockett $60,000. Crockett was fronting to him at the time, which meant he was bringing him a lot of pot and not getting paid for it until it was sold to someone else. Fronting was a pretty common arrangement in the industry, though it required a level of trust beyond the norm. Back when the economy was still strong, Crockett would usually get his money within a week and a half, no problem. Until the day he went to get paid and there was a problem. A girl arrived. He was expecting $75,000, and she didn't have the money. She explained that a driver had gotten busted in

Arizona. The police had confiscated the pot and the money. Now, Crockett's connection could have shrugged it off and walked away; sometimes people got busted and did just that. But this guy didn't. It was the honor of the outlaw. He sold some property and eventually paid Crockett back.

In the meantime, under that same code of honor, Crockett had to come up with money to give to the people whose product he had fronted. He began making payments to them until the rest of the money came through. If he didn't, he knew that trust in him would be shattered and he'd never be able to work in the industry again.

Crockett's connection had paid him back by now, so a couple of weeks earlier Crockett had started working with the guy again. But only with cash up front—no more credit. Since he started back, Crockett had made $8,000 running loads to the city, just like this one.

The Mitsubishi passed through the Waldo Tunnel, just before the bridge, and emerged into an only-in-San-Francisco view. On this hot August evening, when temperatures in the North Bay were still hovering in the eighties, San Francisco's famous fog was rolling over the bridge so quickly it looked like steam bubbling out of a kettle. A thick band of mist had already moved across the bay, shrouding the water in a cottony veil that made the art deco downtown skyline in the distance look as though it were floating on a cloud.

"Ahh, I'm going in!" Crockett yelled, as he drove into fog that was so dense he couldn't see the bridge's trademark orange towers ahead.

The idea was to get in and get out.

Crockett didn't like to linger when he was moving weight, or other people's money.

In a residential neighborhood in the shadow of Sutro Tower, he pulled the Mitsubishi to a stop. He popped his trunk, pulled out the Watershed bag with the ten pounds of weed in it, and strolled down the sidewalk toward a nondescript row house. Crockett's connection wasn't home. Instead, a cute young girl handed him a paper bag that contained a box with $24,000 in cash inside. The bills were secured with rubber bands in $5,000 and $1,000 bundles. Crockett left the Watershed bag with the pot. The cute girl offered him a hit off her bong. It was tempting, but for once, Crockett refused.

People were waiting.

Crockett had just made it back over the bridge when his phone rang. It was his connection, telling him he'd be calling again in a couple of days.

"Coolio," Crockett replied.

When that call came in, Crockett would get in touch with his grower friends, as he had earlier that evening. They used code words to discuss price and amount over the phone. Earlier, for instance, Crockett said he knew a contract worker who paid "$24 an hour," which was $2,400 a pound. Often, given his proximity to wine country, he'd use wine terms. "Ten bottles of wine" would be ten pounds. In Humboldt, telephone code for pounds ranged from "firewood" to "puppies" to "produce," or even "quilt squares."

The speed limit on the highway in front of the Frank

Lloyd Wright–designed Marin Civic Center was fifty-five. The Mitsubishi's speedometer hovered at seventy, then eighty. He zipped across three lanes in seconds, happy to be out of city traffic. The scanner on the windshield sounded one long beep.

"Laser alert," its computerized voice announced.

Crockett downshifted and moved into a slower lane. Within minutes, he passed three highway patrol cars.

The last ticket Crockett had been given was just before Christmas. He was going seventy-four in the rain near his house. The fine came to over $800, including the fix-it portion for his funky muffler. He managed to fight it. When it came down to it, Crockett knew he drove like an asshole, and he knew that the money he was carrying could be taken from him if he got pulled over. Sometimes he'd even feel a little guilty about it. He knew he wouldn't be able to drive the way he did if he were black or Latino, because studies showed their rates of being searched by police were so much higher. He also knew he abused his commercial license because every time he got pulled over, the police officer would ask what it was for, and when he told them he was a firefighter, more often than not, they'd let him go.

The guilt never made him stop, though. For Crockett, the government was corrupt and the system was broken. Whenever his money from Frankie did come through, he planned to spend it building that cabin on the commune. It was nothing more than a foundation now, but Crockett pictured a simple little place where he could retreat and grow vegetables when everything fell apart. It was his own spin on the Back-to-the-Land dream, a remembrance of his childhood.

Soon, Crockett was back on a country road again. The sun was starting to set, and the sky was streaked with orange. It looked like he was driving into a watercolor.

When he pulled up in front of his house, he revved his engine, gunned the car forward, and jerked up the emergency brake. The car spun around 180 degrees, *Dukes of Hazzard* style, coming to a sudden stop next to a white fence and a grassy pasture.

Later, between bong hits, Crockett would weigh the cash, divide it, and vacuum-seal it in plastic bags, before heading out on the last mission of the day: to deliver it to the growers. But first, he would take a long, hot shower and let the dirt wash off him, swirling brown around the drain.

The life of the outlaw remained pretty much the same after the vote, just as it did for the deputy sheriff responsible for enforcing the laws. A year later, voters in Colorado and Washington approved marijuana legalization for recreational use in their states. It wasn't immediately obvious how that would work, or what the reaction from the Obama administration would be as this issue of states' rights continued to play out, but one thing was sure: as long as marijuana remained illegal in some states and unregulated on a national level, the black market would live on, and the Crocketts of the world would continue to work in it. In California, it would turn out, life changed most of all for an old-time grower who had hoped to step out into the light and become a legitimate member of society.

CHAPTER NINETEEN

Mare

Late one April morning, when the cherry trees around Mare's deck were covered in pale pink blossoms, and it seemed that, after endless months of rain and snow, spring had finally arrived for good, Len came for coffee. He was the same Len whom Mare had first laid eyes on back at the Haight-Ashbury Post Office all those decades ago, the man with whom she had moved to this place in a truck called Beast, though time had left its mark on him, too. His beard was more salt than pepper now, but he was still the love of Mare's life, even though she knew they could never live together.

Len had stayed in the area, too. He lived just down the road, and he had become like family to Mare over the years. Like all older people, sometimes they'd get together and talk about how much things had changed. Len's young neighbors, for instance, had never heard of the 1960s radical revolutionary group known as the Weather Underground.

On this day, however, Len had come to check on Mare and see how she was adjusting to her recent loss, one that would affect every aspect of her life moving forward. They sat and drank coffee, and looked out on the butter-yellow daffodils that were blooming in buckets on Mare's deck and talked about how her younger sister, Ellen, had died that past month.

The sisters were close. Ellen never was a hippie, even though Mare and all her friends were. Mare liked to tell the story about how the only time Ellen ever smoked pot, she rear-ended a Volkswagen. Ellen had lived down in Berkeley, and worked as a flight attendant for decades. She'd also owned a house near Mare on the Mattole River. Since neither sister had children or a husband, they had planned to live together and take care of each other during their Golden Years.

In February, Ellen had called Mare and asked what she wanted for her seventy-first birthday, which was coming up later that month.

"For you to come up and visit," Mare told her.

A few days later, Ellen called back and said she had been overcome by a strange fatigue and wouldn't be able to make it after all. At the end of that week, Ellen asked Mare to come down and stay with her while doctors ran some tests. It took them a while to find the cancer in her pancreas. They offered Ellen chemo, but when she found out it wouldn't save her life, only prolong it for a bit, she told them to cut the bracelets off her wrists and take the needles out of her arm. She was going home. The doctors gave her four days to two months.

She had four days.

They set up a bed for her in the living room. Like at Mare's cabin, Ellen's home in the Berkeley Hills had a wall of windows that filled the space with light, but her view was decidedly different. It looked out onto the gray-blue San Francisco Bay, and the Golden Gate Bridge that stretched above the water in the distance.

Mare went through the house and collected photographs of the people whom Ellen loved and had passed before her, like the old guy with the cigar who had been a union rep at the airline. Mare placed the photos around the foot of Ellen's bed. She told Ellen that the people in the photos were waiting for her.

"I don't want to go to heaven," Ellen said.

"What?!" Mare shrieked.

"Because I'll have to be with all those idiot Tea Party people."

Both sisters laughed.

"If you can," Mare asked her, "when you get to wherever you go, will you try to send us a message?"

Ellen said she would try.

The night Ellen died, Mare and the three others who were taking turns as round-the-clock caregivers threw a party and invited all of Ellen's friends who lived nearby. Ellen couldn't talk that day, but everyone gathered around and traded stories about her. A few hours after the party ended, the caregiver who was also a trained nurse noticed that Ellen's breaths were coming slower and further apart. Mare and others gathered at her bedside, sang to her, and took turns saying their good-byes. Ellen's eyes were open, and she looked at them as they sang, "Fly away little bird, fly high, fly free."

Mare didn't realize that Ellen had taken her last breath until there wasn't another one.

And then grief came like a dark wave and pulled Mare out to sea.

A few hours later, a floor lamp with a pink shade that Ellen had made flickered on in the living room. It stayed on for four days before it shut off for good. Mare took it as a sign from Ellen that she got where she was going.

In those first surreal days following her sister's death, Mare learned that Ellen had managed to become a millionaire on her flight attendant's salary, and she had left it all to Mare. When they were growing up, Ellen used to sit with their father and play stocks, whereas when Mare learned about numbers, her eyes would glaze over. Mare inherited four houses: two in Berkeley, one in Humboldt, and the family cabin back on Beaver Island, in Michigan. There were also bank accounts, stocks, and money Ellen had loaned friends.

All in all, the whole thing felt entirely overwhelming, and Mare wasn't sure how to deal with it. Suddenly she found herself spending all her time toting an attaché case around to law and investment offices in Berkeley. She was also unsure of her feelings about this newfound wealth. The life she had carved out for herself in Humboldt was a simple one. She had her little annuity, and her Social Security from teaching sculpture classes. She had just enough. It wasn't cushy, but Mare was proud that she wasn't one of those peo-ple who kept wanting more. In a way, she'd never outgrown the sixties. She wanted a simple, happy life. She'd never developed the "greed gene," as she called it. She was com-fortable, and that was that.

Now, suddenly, she was an heiress.

One thing was clear: Mare certainly didn't need to grow pot anymore to supplement her income. She could retire from growing for good. But she decided to do just the op-posite. Not only did she decide to keep growing, but in the wake of her sister's death, she decided to throw herself into getting out the word about the importance of mari-juana grown sustainably in the sun. The plant had been so good to Mare, and had helped provide her with a life she loved. She sort of worshipped it when it was grown outdoors, and thought it was just sad for people to put it under lights and treat it with pesticides. She thought it somehow stunted their appreciation of the plant and their own literal growth.

After the vote, Mare read a cover story in *Mother Jones* magazine that solidified her opinion. The article focused on two young entrepreneurs who were attempting to build a marijuana supply store franchise that they wanted to become the "Walmart of Weed." One was a Morgan Stan-ley investment banker, the other a twenty-six-year-old Lamborghini-driving son of a taxi tycoon. They wore suits and spoke of IPOs and reality TV shows. They did not seem to be in the business for the love of the plant. In the article, the twenty-six-year-old said that the older generation were brilliant scientists, but they weren't such brilliant businessmen. After reading the *Mother Jones* article, Mare didn't know if it was just plain ignorance or if there was an actual conspiracy, but she wasn't about to let young men like this, who were still in diapers back when she was running from the helicopters, co-opt this industry. She decided then and there to invest her time and money into getting the word out about sun-grown marijuana, for the sake of the environment and her community.

She began by passing out flyers at the Berkeley Farmers' Market that carried messages such as "How Green is *Your* Green?"

The flyers came from a Humboldt group called Grow It in the Sun. The group of environmentally conscious growers had formed in the Salmon Creek community in 2008, running ads on local radio stations and in local papers to raise awareness about the environmental dangers of indoor marijuana grows, including the off-the-grid kind that were powered by diesel generators and had become widespread in the Humboldt Hills during the CAMP years. The generators were noisy and hungry, and emitted carbon dioxide into the air. Sometimes the fuel used to power them leaked into local creeks. Now that there was a medical law providing growers with a cloak of protection, the folks at Grow It in the Sun encouraged people to move their plants back outside, "as nature intended."

In April 2011, a study was released that gave Grow It in the Sun some serious credibility. Dr. Evan Mills is a government scientist, and a member of the Intergovernmental

Panel on Climate Change (IPCC), the international body of scientists who would share the 2007 Nobel Peace Prize with Al Gore. One day, Mills began to notice all the indoor gardening stores popping up everywhere, and when he took a look inside, he saw that they were selling more fans, lights, and other devices than soil and fertilizer. On his own time, Mills decided to look a little closer at how much energy all that equipment was consuming, and discovered in the process that indoor pot growing sucks up a lot of electricity—9 percent of all household use in California, to be precise, and 2 percent of household use nationally.

Those impossibly bright lights used to grow plants inside were the same intensity as the lights in an operating room, Mills found. That is five hundred times more powerful than a reading lamp. His study, "Energy Up in Smoke: The Carbon Footprint of Indoor Cannabis Production," found that the amount of energy used to grow pot indoors nationwide created the same amount of greenhouse gas emissions as three million cars. Mills's study blew up online, and received attention in the national and international press.

Mare already knew that growing plants under lights was wasteful and wrong, but now that the media were paying some attention to the matter, thanks to Mills's report, she wondered if the dispensaries that sold this indoor marijuana might also begin to look at things a little differently. Mare had met Stephen DeAngelo recently, at the *High Times*–sponsored Cannabis Cup in San Francisco. With his skinny long braids and bowler hats, DeAngelo looked something like a hippie leprechaun. He also happened to be one of the owners of Harborside Health Center in Oakland, which billed itself as the world's largest medical marijuana dispensary. At the Cannabis Cup, Mare told DeAngelo that he cut into her market and that he needed to focus more on outdoor pot. He seemed sympathetic, and Mare got the impression that she could e-mail him and stop by sometime. It sounded great, except that he didn't return any of her e-mails. So Mare decided to go down and check out Harborside in person.

───────

Harborside Health Center is located in a nondescript business park on the Oakland waterfront, just down the freeway from the port where shipping containers are stacked like LEGOs and the giant cranes used to unload them define the city's skyline. There's no sign out front advertising the dispensary. There is only the address: 1840, painted in big black letters on the side of the building.

On the warm summer day when Mare visited, she wore flip-flops and a long pink sundress, and she hobbled toward the entrance carrying a paper bag filled with a pound of pot from her past harvest, which she hoped to sell after attending a new vendor orientation. A beefy but gentle security guard told her that she wasn't allowed to consume any medicine on site, and to please be respectful of the neighbors in nearby offices as she passed through a metal detector and entered the dispensary.

To the right was the sales area, which was centered on

a long counter where samples of various marijuana strains were displayed in glass cases. Friendly salespeople attended to the dispensary's customers—ringing up $22 million in annual sales. Mare loved the look of the place. She found it clean, modern, and colorful, with just a touch of hippie.

She had already come the day before to fill out the necessary paperwork and show her doctor's recommendation, so she was led straight through to the vendors' waiting room. Mare had also inspected the competition that previous day and was unimpressed. Of the twenty-five varieties of marijuana for sale at the dispensary when she visited, only one was grown outside. Of course it went for about half of what the stuff grown indoors was going for, but it didn't even smell good. Mare had turned up her nose after giving it a sniff.

The waiting room was empty. Mare hobbled around and took in her surroundings. She stopped to admire a peace sign that was made out of bent twigs. Upon closer inspection, she was pleased to realize it was made out of hemp stalks. On a table in the corner was a little wooden sculpture of a woman doing a backbend.

"Ah, Balinese art!" she cooed, before plunking herself down in a leather chair underneath a wall of framed articles about Harborside, many of which featured the face of DeAngelo. There were articles from *The New York Times*, and a framed cover of *Fortune* magazine with Mary-Louise Parker from *Weeds* on the cover. "Is Pot Already Legal?" it asked.

At Harborside it definitely felt like it.

As Mare looked around and waited, more people trickled in, including a clean-cut young couple who looked like they'd just strolled off the Berkeley campus. A few minutes later, a portly fortysomething man carrying a duffel bag plunked himself down in a chair near the door. Then came a young man with saggy pants and a messy Afro, and a twentysomething earthy-crunchy girl. Of the eight vendors who eventually showed up for the orientation about selling their marijuana to the dispensary, Mare was the only senior citizen.

Eventually a door swung open and a woman who appeared to be in her late thirties, with flowing red hair and black knee boots, strolled into the room. In a soft, velvety voice, she introduced herself as Caroline and explained that she worked in purchasing. Then she began a spiel that she must have given hundreds of times before, about what they were looking to buy at Harborside. The dispensary purchased top-shelf pot for $3,600 a pound. Mid-grade to lower-grade marijuana, which included anything grown in the sun, was worth less, around $2,000 a pound. Not that sun-grown isn't good, Caroline said, it's just that customers weren't willing to pay more than $30 an eighth for it.

In her hand Caroline held a clear plastic turkey bag full of trimmed green buds of a strain called Boggle Gum. It was an example of what she was looking for.

"It smells really good and shiny and beautiful," she said, before passing the bag around so everyone could take a closer look.

"Patients can't touch it," she said, "so it's gotta smell good."

The pot also had to be trimmed tightly, and all small buds had to be removed from the bags.

"If it can fit up your nose," she said, "take it out."

Then it was show-and-tell time, and from out of the backpacks and purses and, in Mare's case, paper bags, everyone pulled out their plastic turkey bags of pot or lumps of hash.

When it was Mare's turn, Caroline opened the bag, thrust her face inside, and inhaled.

"I call it Bubble Bath," Mare told her. "It's a mix of Stinky Pinky and Bubble Gum."

"Where did you get the Stinky Pinky?" Caroline asked.

"I'm from Humboldt County, and we have it there."

Caroline asked Mare to stay after; while one by one she rejected all the other pot that had been brought in that day.

"This is so nice," Caroline said, as she smelled Mare's pot again. "You grew this outdoors?"

She then picked up individual buds, prying the little flowers apart, inspecting the orange resiny hairs, and looking for mold.

"I did, and I call it Bubble Bath," Mare said, "because it's not like it puts you to sleep; it just relaxes you."

"Well, how much do you want for it?"

"Oh, I want top dollar, of course."

"Well, throw out a number."

"We lost our market to you guys. I saw Steve at the Cannabis Cup and I told him that."

"I think I could do twenty-one hundred. What do you think?"

"Oh, I don't know," Mare hemmed and hawed a little.

"I could go as high as twenty-two hundred."

"Okay, I'll get you higher next time," Mare said. "Come on, we started all of this. We know how to grow. We're the marijuana moonshiners."

And so Mare left her pot and was handed a slip of paper. The dispensary would run some lab tests, to check its THC levels and ensure it didn't contain any mold. Then, if all went well, in a week's time Mare would have an envelope with $2,200 cash waiting for her.

When she was back outside, a few minutes later, Mare clapped her hands with glee.

"Oh, I'm so happy!" she cried out. "That's exactly how I wanted it to go!"

A week later, she knelt down by the waters of Lake Michigan and scattered some of her sister Ellen's ashes.

———

The first rain came in early September out at the coast. Mare's neighbors called it the year of the perfect storm because everyone had such big beautiful crops but then had to throw half of it away because of the mold. Mare lost a lot of her crop to mold, too. It came sneaking into her drying room when she wasn't looking and rotted the hanging buds from the inside out. The mold was unlike any she had ever seen before: it was gray and kind of cobwebby. Mare found it kind of pretty, even though she'd swear whenever she found it and had to discard an entire cola.

The crop that survived had pink hairs and smelled like

cherries and Bazooka bubble gum. Mare and one of the guys at the Tea House Collective decided to call it Sour Pink, because it sounded like a cocktail. Mare sold a pound or two of it to Harborside Health Center and spent a day at the dispensary talking to patients on behalf of her collective. She felt a bit like a unicorn there; so many people told her that they had heard of the old marijuana moonshiners up in Humboldt but had never actually met one. Mare saw healthy young guys coming in looking for heavy-THC pot, and she saw the medical patients: the Iraqi vet who used marijuana to help with the phantom pains he'd have in his missing limb, and the woman with the scar down her face who said it helped with the headaches she had had ever since she was in a bad car accident. Mare wasn't sure what the future of pot growing held, but figured she'd just carve out her niche growing a small amount of *sativa* in the sun. She had also been reading about a nonpsychoactive molecule found in pot called cannabidiol, or CBD, which was shown to have strong anti-inflammatory qualities. She was going to try to breed more of this into her crop, and hoped that everyone would eventually catch up.

Meanwhile, she began to think about growing older. After Ellen died, Mare had to have her knee replaced, and there were a few uncomfortable weeks where she couldn't drive. When she had first moved to the Southern Humboldt community, Mare and her friends used to lament the fact that they didn't have any elders among them. Now they were the elders. William, the younger man who lived on her property and helped her with chores, joked that he was going to get a van and name it Daisy and he'd drive Mare and all her old friends around in it.

Late one afternoon, William came over and got Mare stoned on some of the Sour Pink. After he left, she lay down on her bed and gazed out the window above her kitchen sink, which looked out on the tree line. Just beyond it, the continent came to an end and the ocean and the sky stretched into the horizon. Mare lay there and watched the sun set for what felt like hours. She realized that her knees weren't hurting her anymore, and she felt relaxed and happy. They'd really nailed it with the crop this year. Mare felt great, and when she fell asleep that night, she would sleep soundly for the first time in a long while. Outside, the sky burned orange and then a brilliant pink, and the dark silhouette of the trees out the window were backlit shadows, like a Magritte painting. The sun slowly slipped behind the ocean, and everything faded gently into night.

AUTHOR'S REMARKS

I was born and raised in Northern California just south of the region known as the Emerald Triangle. In Napa and Sonoma, where I grew up, wine grapes are the cash crop, but marijuana is still part of the local culture and economy. My parents weren't growers, but they were members of the counterculture, and when I was little they would take me to parties that in my memory were a blur of laughter, long skirts, scratchy beards, and the sweet, heady scent of marijuana. Since childhood, it is a smell I have associated with adults having a good time.

As I grew older, I became aware of the gamble people took to work in the lucrative underground economy. When I was fourteen, my best friend's father went to prison for growing marijuana. Her sense of secrecy and shame was so strong that I didn't learn until the last minute that the FBI had seized her family's home and that her father was going away for five years. I happened to be sleeping over that night. In the morning, I stood awkwardly in the hallway as my friend's father hugged her good-bye. She walked into her bedroom and quietly shut the door. At the other end of the hallway, her little brother sobbed.

That was in 1990. In 2010, when I moved home after five years in New York, I discovered that growers weren't going to jail like before, and their underground economy was speedily going mainstream, complete with marijuana trade shows and city permits for pot delivery services. Now that seemingly anyone could grow pot under the medical marijuana law, I wondered what all this meant for the notorious pot towns I'd heard about up north, like Laytonville in Mendocino and Garberville in Humboldt. What was a pot town? How does a place become one? And how were all these changes to the industry affecting them?

I decided to see if I could answer some of these questions. Originally, I thought I was doing research for a book on how California legalized marijuana, and I figured whatever was happening up north would be part of that story. I had been to the area before to see the big trees, but I knew nothing of the culture. When I crossed the redwood curtain and arrived in Humboldt that summer, I had no idea I was entering another world and that what I found there would become the story. I quickly realized that the only way to understand this world and earn the trust of the people who lived there was to become part of it. I originally went to Humboldt for a week. I left more than a year later.

The entire time I lived in southern Humboldt County, I was always open about who I was: a journalist at work on a book about the community. Despite the ominous reputation of Humboldt growers in the mass media—the armed and dangerous renegade ready to shoot anyone who ventures on their property—I never really felt unsafe. Granted, I was asked three times if I was law enforcement by younger, paranoid types, but I saw only one gun. In general,

I was welcomed with incredible warmth and acceptance. After years of living in secrecy, many elder members of the community were especially eager to share their stories. And what stories they shared: how they discovered their cash crop by accident, hid from helicopters, and built a community with their bare hands. In an era when small farming had all but disappeared, Humboldt pot growers earned a decent and sometimes great living working the land in a breathtakingly beautiful place. It was an American Dream of sorts. There were often moments when life there reminded me of a Norman Rockwell painting, with a big, leafy marijuana plant towering in the background, like the time I attended a school fund-raiser where pot smoke hung in the air, and a man auctioned off nylon bags for making hashish alongside baskets of homegrown tomatoes and hand-knit scarves.

Early on, I realized that I couldn't tell the story of the place through just one person, so I focused on four people who represent different aspects of marijuana culture: Crockett represented the younger, business-minded grower who had come to Humboldt to make money. Mare was the woman who'd planted the seeds that helped start the industry and who never gave up on her hippie ideals. Emma had been raised in the community and decided early on it wasn't worth the risk to grow. And like someone out of an old Western, Bob was a deputy sheriff in a town of outlaws.

I witnessed many of the events described in this book. Some scenes were recounted to me during interviews and supplemented with court documents, news reports, and second-source interviews. Many of the spoken words were uttered in my presence. Other quotes were confirmed whenever possible. The statements of Mikal Wilde, whose lawyers declined to let him speak with me due to his ongoing legal case, are paraphrased based on a reliable source.

The majority of my reporting took place while spending open-ended days and nights with my subjects. We went to the grocery store, cooked dinner, went to parties, worked in the garden, and, in the case of Bob, patrolled the area. In addition to my main characters, to have a deeper understanding of the area and culture I conducted interviews with dozens of other community members. Sometimes it felt as though I had interviewed the whole town.

During my time in the community, I straddled the role of outsider and insider. To make ends meet, I found a job serving wine and crepes at a local jazz club and café. Even though I didn't work directly in the industry, I understood that marijuana money indirectly paid my salary too.

While I lived in Southern Humboldt, I got lost on dirt roads, cooled off in the Eel River on summer days, hunted for mushrooms, fell under the spell of the redwoods, and made wonderful friends with people who, of course, grew pot. I saw how this income enabled them to pursue their dreams, but I came to believe that their economy is built upon something that is wrong—not the marijuana itself, but the fact that medical laws aside, it is still fundamentally illegal. For the readers who wonder about my stance on the issue, here it is: I believe that marijuana should be legal and regulated, for the economy, for the environment, for civil rights, for Mexico, and to end the violence associated with its illegality. No one should ever die over a plant that doesn't kill people.

With the passing of the recent recreational use laws in Colorado and Washington, and as more states approve medical marijuana, it looks like the long, slow march toward legalization will continue. If that happens, someday the story of the people whom Mare calls the marijuana moonshiners will be just a footnote in history, and this book will ultimately be just a snapshot in time of a place called Humboldt.

ACKNOWLEDGMENTS

Writing a book is an enormous leap of faith, and many times, when mine felt close to running out, I drew on the support of a large community of friends and my family to keep me going. My gratitude goes out to everyone who helped me along the way. Endless thanks to Somer Huntley and Andy Solomon for the use of the house in Whitethorn that started me on this journey. Alicia Skuce generously loaned me her apartment in Oakland one summer. For many years, Claudia Schuster's backroom has been my refuge in San Francisco, and I am eternally grateful for that space and her friendship. Ferren Knickerbocker hosted me in Eureka. Heather Sarantis and Robert Collier gave me an office in Berkeley, and their amazing son, Dylan, brightened my writing breaks. Susan Mazur graciously allowed me to use her yurt as my Redway office. Mark and Marcia provided me with the most amazing gift of a house on the beach in Mexico, and I am forever grateful to them both. My heartfelt thanks to Doreen Puentes in Garberville, who provided me with a room to rent, and the occasional glass of wine and encouraging pat on the back.

I feel tremendous gratitude for my father, Paul Brady, and my stepmother, Kathleen, for the use of the Subaru during those rainy winter months and for carving out a space for me in St. Helena one last time. Thank you to my mother, Elizabeth, and my stepfather, Greg Schimpf, for love and support and for coming north to see the trees with me.

I am lucky to have many wonderful supportive friends. In particular, Jenny Hole, whom I have known for so long, provided constant laughter and pep talks while I wrote this book and made me an honorary aunt to beautiful Stella Lou. I don't know what I would have done without Brooke Bundgard, who welcomed me to Oakland with love and light, and cheered me on as I raced toward the finish line. Jordan Rosenfeld has followed my path from our walks along D Street, to New York, and back. She graciously read several drafts, encouraged me every step of the way, and sent a last-minute writer's first-aid kit. Anya Roberts-Toney also read multiple drafts, cheered me on, and has an eye for detail for which I am incredibly grateful. Jennifer Bleyer was there to talk things through and offered feedback that helped make this a better book. I look forward to returning the favor. Megan Feldman supported me with her laughter, encouragement, and last-minute edits.

I am infinitely grateful to my agent, Larry Weissman, and his wife Sascha Alper, for guiding me through this process and for pushing me to follow the story further than I was comfortable in the beginning, which helped me discover something all the richer. Immense gratitude to my editor, Ben Greenberg, for betting on me in the first place, for suggesting I step out of the story, and for his patience with my over-reporting. Enormous thanks as well to the amazing team at Grand Central who helped usher this book into the world: Liz Connor, Erica Warren, Peggy Holm, Caitlin Mulrooney-Lyski, and Jenna Dolan, whose sharp eye helped save me from my mistakes.

In Mexico, *muchísimas gracias* to the people of Troncones, Guerrero, where the first draft of this book was written. Suzanne and Bob French provided me with many lovely dinners there, and hosted Christmas at their home in Tamasopo. Thank you to the *maripositas* at the primary school for sweetening my afternoons, and to Beto for the surf and life lessons.

Of all the people I am indebted to for helping make this book possible, the people of southern Humboldt County are at the top of the list. They are some of the most independent people I have ever known, and many of them graciously invited me into their gardens and lives. This book would be empty without them. Thank you to everyone who took the time to share their stories. I am grateful to Liz and Charley for the hospitality and kindness when I first arrived. Mikal Jakubal put up with my city-girl ways, endlessly tried to pin the Jell-O to the wall with me, brought snacks on our bike rides along the Avenue, and never ceased to challenge me to think differently. Marcia Murphy was always there to lend support, to listen, and to have adventures with. Rick Klein and Peter Childs kindly helped me understand the history of the Back-to-the-Land movement. Jeff Hedin taught me to tell the difference between redwood trees and Douglas firs from a distance. Kym Kemp is one of the busiest women I know but was always graciously willing to take a moment to help me understand the community and place that she holds so dear.

I thank Sergeant Kenny Swithenbank and Sheriff Michael Downey of the Humboldt County Sheriff's Department. I am also incredibly grateful for the magical Holly Sweet, who provided me with a job when I was in need of one and became my teacher along the way. And Susan Mazur became like family. Thanks to Prescott Smith for the fresh flowers, the CSA deliveries, and for being such a skillful chauffeur along those treacherous Mexican highways.

And last, but certainly not least, I owe my deepest gratitude to Mare, Emma, Bob, and Crockett. Without their willingness to allow me into their lives, this book would never have been possible. I am grateful to Mare Abidon for her optimism and for standing up for her beliefs. Emma Worldpeace inspired me with her integrity and her friendship. Bob Hamilton taught me about resilience and reminded me of the importance of being able to laugh in the face of adversity. I owe a huge debt to Crockett for his trust and openness. The commercial growers were the hardest to access, and without his participation a crucial part of this tale would have been left untold. While the telling of this story is my own, I hope it honors their trust, honesty, and generosity.

INDEX

Abidon, Ellen, 62, 228–31
Abidon, Mary Em "Mare," 3–15,
    58–73, 116–25, 151–63,
    227–40
  art education of, 59–60
  background of, 61–63
  banking system of, 157–58
  death of sister Ellen, 228–31
  at Gopherville, 60–61, 67–69
  living space of, 155–57
  in marijuana collective,
    159–61, 181
  marijuana crop harvesting by,
    151–52, 155–56, 158–59,
    238–39
  marijuana cultivation of, 73,
    116–17, 151–59, 231–40
  marijuana legalization and,
    10–15, 123–24, 178,
    180–81, 190
  marijuana seeds of, 152–55
  at post-marijuana economy fo-
    rum, 4, 8–15
  protest against Green Sweep,
    120, 122–23
  at Renaissance fairs, 69, 73
  in San Francisco, 58–59, 227
  sun-grown marijuana and,
    161–63, 232–40
ACLU (American Civil Liber-
    ties Union), 185–86
Afghanistan, seeds from, 154
Aia (Emma's sister), 41–43, 44,
    74–75, 78–81, 165–66,
    209
Akselsen, Sean, 84–88, 99,
    128–29
alcohol, 30, 42–43, 132, 167
alcohol prohibition, 167, 184
Allison, Dorothy, 83–84
AmeriCorps, 131
Amsterdam, seeds from, 153,
    155
Anderson, Mary Siler, 100
Antioch College, 62
appellation, 13–14
army's arrival in Southern Hum-
    boldt, 119–25

Back-to-the-Land, x, 61, 65–68
"Ballad of Shadrack" (song),
    81–82

Bank of the Woods, defined, x

Bastard Out of Carolina (Allison), 83

Bear Canyon Bridge, 54

Beginnings in Briceland, 87–88, 159

Benbow, 198, 200

Bennett, William, 120

Berkeley Farmers' Market, 232

Berti, Patrick, 28–29

black market prices, 10–13

Black Oak Ranch, 105–6

Blitzer, Wolf, 189

Blue Sky (dispensary), 182

Bob Hamilton. *See* Hamilton, Bob

Boggle Gum, 236–37

Brown, Jerry, 187, 192

Bubble Gum, 155, 237

Burger, Joey, 114–15

Bush, George H. W., 119–20

California Beer and Beverage Distributors, 187

California Redwood Company, 200–201

Camo Cowboys, 81–82

CAMP (Campaign Against Marijuana Planting), x, 76–79, 124–25, 179, 201

Campbell, Joseph, 61

"CAMP'ed," x, 76–77

cannabidiol (CBD), 239

Cannabis Cup, 21, 233–34

Cannabis Eradication and Reclamation Team (CERT), 201

cannabis indica, 21–22, 154

cannabis sativa, 21–22, 153–55

Caroline (Harborside worker), 236–38

cartels, defined, x

Cato Institute, 26

Chico State School of Social Work, 205–6

Christina, drug death of, 170–76

chronic freedom, 137

Cinderella "Cindra," and Christina's death, 172–73, 174

Civil Liberties Monitoring Project, 179

climate change, 232–33

clones, 152–53

"coconut telegraph," 99

Cohen, Matthew, 211

Coker, Madeline "Maddie," 128

Colorado

marijuana legalization, 226, 245

medical marijuana law, 112

communes (communal living), 67–69

Compassionate Use Act of 1996, 25

Conn, Keith, 143–46, 150, 170, 202

Controlled Substances Act of 1970, 10–11

corporatization of marijuana industry, 13, 26–27, 52, 115, 184

couch lock, 154

Crawford, Eugene, 28, 76

crime. See murders

criminal justice system, 185–87, 193

Crockett Randall. See Randall, Crockett

Custer, Charley, 8

Davis, Kathy, 29, 117–18

Dazey's Supply, 91, 196

Deal, Rod, 124

DeAngelo, Stephen, 233–34, 235

death penalty, 209–10

deaths among youth in southern Humboldt County, 85–89, 128–29, 131–33

Del Real, Max, 115

Democracy Now! (radio program), 26, 178–79

"depping," x, 22

diesel dope. See also indoor-grown marijuana

defined, xi

dirt roads of Humboldt, 141–42

Do Not Resuscitate (DNR) order, 170

Douglas Fir, 154

Downey, Michael, 199, 201

drug cartels, 182, 185

Drug Enforcement Agency (DEA), 76, 211

drug overdoses, 170–76

Drug Policy Alliance, 186

Durkin, Jim, 68–69

Earthdance, 105–6

Edwards, Blossom, 118–19, 125

Eel River, 1–2, 18, 66, 172

Eel River Conservation Camp, 47–48, 53–54

Eichen, Craig, 89

Elders, Joycelyn, 185

Emerald Triangle, 6

Emma Worldpeace. See Worldpeace, Emma

Ethan (Emma's boyfriend), 34–35, 37, 164–65, 167–68, 191, 205, 206, 213–15

Eureka, 57, 64, 96

Firestone, Robert, 92, 202

Fox, Vicente, 185

Frame, Delbert, 72–73

Frankie (Crockett's boss), 22, 23–26, 30, 32–33, 105, 106, 108–10, 189, 192, 219–20, 221, 225

Franti, Michael, 105
Frech, Stephen "EZ Out,"
    38–41, 214
fronting, xi, 222–23
Frye, Mary Elizabeth, 129

Gallegos, Paul, 114, 177, 208
Garberville, 48–50, 66, 71–72,
    91–93, 140–41
Garberville Motel, 200
Garza, Kaleb, 85, 88–89
Gene (Mare's ex-husband), 59,
    62–63
Giauque, Chris, 86–87
Glenn E. Dyer Detention Facil-
    ity, 211–14
God's Pussy, 21
Gopherville, 60–61, 67–69
Gore, Al, 233
Green Rush, 17
Green Sweep Operation,
    119–25
grower, defined, xi
Grow It in the Sun, 232–33
grow or scene, defined, xi
guerrilla growing, xi, 116

Haag, Melinda, 210–11
Haight-Ashbury, 59, 227
Haight-Ashbury Post Office, 58,
    227
Hamilton, Anna "Banana," 4, 8,
    10–14

Hamilton, Bob, 47–57, 90–104,
    139–50, 170–77, 195–204
    background of, 95–97
    Christina's drug death and,
        170–76
    in harassment mode, 139–41
    home invasions and, 198,
        199–200
    job departure date for,
        195–96, 203–4
    job reassignment of, 200–204
    marijuana industry and, 50–57,
        91–92, 94–95, 97–98,
        142–43, 147–50, 196–98
    marijuana legalization and,
        52–53, 176–77, 179,
        191–92, 194
    marijuana smugglers and,
        51–52, 196–98
    outstanding arrest warrants
        and, 141–47
    on patrols, 54–57, 90–95,
        97–104, 139–41, 201–4
    transients and, 48–50, 54–57,
        139–41, 196
Hamilton, Jessica, 195
Harbin Hot Springs, 162
Harborside Health Center
    (Oakland), 234–38, 239
Harding, Tonya, 146
Harte, Bret, 64, 101
helicopters, 75–76, 77, 117, 127
Hemp Connection, 51, 91

hempheimers, defined, xi
High Times, 48
hipneck, defined, xi
history of Humboldt County,
  63–65
Holder, Eric, 194
home invasions, 53, 198–200
homestead, defined, xi
homicides. *See* murders
Huffington Post, 186–87, 193
Huffman, Alice, 186–87
Humboldt, Alexander von, 64
Humboldt County jail, 164,
  167, 212
Humboldt County Sheriff's Office, 29, 48–57, 201. *See also* Hamilton, Bob
Humboldt Growers Association,
  113–15, 177, 202
Humboldt Hemp Fest, 6
Humboldt Hunnies, 91–92
Humboldt Marijuana Eradication Task Force, 179
Humboldt time, defined, xi
Humboldt twenty, defined, xi

indica, 21–22, 154
indoor-grown marijuana, 17, 22,
  52, 161–62, 233–34
Intergovernmental Panel on Climate Change (IPCC),
  232–33

Jameton, John Wyatt, 85–86
Jamison, Delos "Cy," 121–22
Jewel (Mare's cousin), 7, 60
John (Emma's brother), 75,
  78–81
Johnston's Quality Motel,
  92–93
Juan, Robert "Buddha," 103–4
Juarez-Madrid, Mario Roberto,
  36–37, 207–8

Kayla, and Christina's death,
  172, 174–75
Kemp, Kym "Redheaded Blackbelt," 7–8
King Range National Conservation Area, 100–101,
  116–17, 119–20
KMUD-FM, 4, 8, 12, 130–38,
  178–79
Kneeland Shooting, 36–37,
  164–67, 169, 207–8

Land, Brandy, 146–47
LaRue, Nick, 128
Laura Virginia, 64
Law Enforcement Against
  Prohibition (LEAP),
  187–88
Lee, Barbara, 185
Lee, Richard, 181–84
legalization of marijuana. *See* marijuana legalization

INDEX

Lema, Larry, 28–29
Len (Mare's partner), 58–59, 60–61, 63, 67, 69, 73, 227–28
Lewis, Margaret, 130–31, 133–38
Lighthouse Ranch, 68–69
Lisa (Emma's sister), 34–35, 40, 43–44, 74–75, 79–81, 128, 166
Lone Pine Motel, 146–47
Lopez, Fernando, 207–8
Los Angeles Times, 53, 57, 124
Lost Paradise Land Corp., 103–4
Lovelace, Mark, 13
Lucky (dog), 3–4, 178, 190
Lux, Syreeta, 8–10

McKee, Bob, 99–100
McKinleyville, 201
McNamara, Joseph, 188
Mare. *See* Abidon, Mary Em "Mare"
marijuana arrests, 185–87, 193
marijuana culture, radio program on growing up in, 130–38
marijuana debts, 220–21, 222–23
marijuana harvesting, 106–13, 151–52, 155–56, 158–59

marijuana legalization, 10–15
    Bob Hamilton and, 52–53, 176–77
    Crockett and, 26–27, 189–90
    Emma and, 137–38, 167
    Mare and, 10–15, 123–24
marijuana legalization vote (Proposition 19), 178–94
    Bob Hamilton and, 179, 191–92, 194
    failure of vote, 189–94
    Lee and, 181–84
    Mare and, 178, 180–81, 190
    opponents of, 187
    proponents of, 185–88
marijuana names, 21–22
marijuana potency, 33, 69–70, 162
marijuanaries, defined, xi
marijuana seeds, 153–55
marijuana types, 21–22
Mateel Community Center, 5–6, 7–10, 12, 100, 136, 140
Mateel Hemp Fest, 6
Medical Cannabis Ordinance Workshop, 113–15
medical marijuana, 9, 11, 25, 113, 182, 210–11
Miller, Bud, 73
Mills, Evan, 232–33
Milne, A. A., 157
mold, 106, 107–9, 161, 238–39

Moody, Emily, 128
Moore, Conan, 144–50
Morning Glory Manor, 41–42,
    74–76, 78–80
Mother Jones, 193, 231–32
Mothers Against Drunk Driving
    (MADD), 187
murders, 27–30, 35–37, 85–88,
    168–69
Mikal Wilde shooting, 35–37,
    164–67, 207–8

NAACP (National Association
    for the Advancement of
    Colored People), 185–87
names of marijuana, 21–22
Native Americans, 64
Neely, Bonnie, 113–14
New York Times, 71–72, 124–25
Noriega, Manuel, 119
North Coast Journal, 36, 87, 166,
    183

Oaksterdam University, 182,
    211
Obad, Hussain, 200
Obama, Barack, 210–11, 226
O.G. Kush, 21–22, 31–32
Omar (Emma's brother), 41–42,
    44, 74–75, 79–81, 84–85,
    88–89, 164
Operation Green Sweep,
    119–25

Operation Sinsemilla, 76
outdoor-grown marijuana, 22,
    161–62, 231–40
outstanding arrest warrants,
    141–46

Pacific Coast Highway, 101
packaging marijuana, 112
paraquat, 70–71
partnering, 24
Peron, Dennis, 187
Phillipsville, 144, 172
Philp, Gary, 114
"Post-Marijuana Prohibition
    Economy Forum," 4, 8–15
"potstitutes," xi, 92
Prairie Creek Redwoods State
    Park, 203
price support system, for illegal
    marijuana, 10–13
Proposition 19, 178–94
    Bob Hamilton and, 179,
        191–92, 194
    failure of vote, 189–94
    Lee and, 181–84
    Mare and, 178, 180–81, 190
    opponents of, 187
    "Post-Marijuana Prohibition
        Economy Forum," 4, 8–15
    proponents of, 185–88
Proposition 215, 25
provenance of seeds, 153–55

Randall, Crockett, 16–33,
105–13
background of, 22–24
cabin in the woods of, 19–21
marijuana crop harvesting by,
106–13
marijuana crop of, 22, 24–27,
31–33
marijuana legalization and,
26–27, 189–90
transporting marijuana,
112–13, 216–26
violent crime and, 27, 30
RAND Corporation, 12, 33, 183
Rant and Rave (radio show), 8
Reagan, Ronald, 62–63
Red Cross, 204
Redway, 7, 66, 94–95
Redwoods Rural Health Center,
136
redwood trees, 1–2, 64–65
Regulate, Control, and Tax Cannabis Act. See Proposition 19
regulation of marijuana industry,
13, 113–15, 161
Renaissance fairs, 69, 73
Renner, Dave, 124
Richardson Grove State Park,
1–2, 63
Rivas, Linda. See Sage
Riverwood Inn, 144
Rosebud, 163

Sage (Linda Rivas), 37–46,
74–81, 128, 135–36
arrest for growing marijuana,
75–81
birth of Emma, 37–40
growing marijuana, 44–46,
77–80, 135–36
mental health breakdown of,
208–9
Salmon Creek, 40–41
San Francisco Chronicle, 182, 188
sativa, 21–22, 153–55
Schwarzenegger, Arnold, 193
secrecy surrounding marijuana
industry, 6, 23, 45–46,
132–36, 241
seeds, 152–55
Sempervirens, 209
Sensi Seed Bank (Amsterdam),
153, 155
Shelter Cove, 53, 98–99, 101–3
Shelter Cove General Store,
102–3
Shelter Cove Resort Improvement District, 143
Shinn, Rex, 87
Sinkyone Wilderness State
Park, 5
sinsemilla, 69–70
Solar Dan, 196
"Song of the Redwood Tree"
(Whitman), 65
Soros, George, 185

INDEX

Sour Pink, 239, 240

South Fork High School, 83, 85, 127, 128

Steven, and Christina's death, 173, 176–77

Stinky Pinky, 237

Strawberry Creek, 28

sun-grown marijuana, 22, 161–62, 231–40

Swithenbank, Kenny, 48, 54–57, 99

Tea House Collective, 159–61, 163, 181

Thank Jah It's Friday (radio show), 178–79

THC (delta-9-tetrahydro-cannabinol), 70

Tie-Dye Debrah, 39

timber industry, 64–65

transportation of marijuana, 112–13, 216–26

trichomes, 106–7

trimmers, 109–11

Tuohy, Tom, 208

215s, x, 94–95, 148–49

University of California at Berkeley, 59–60, 126–29, 132

violence, 27–30, 35–37, 85–89, 168–69

War on Drugs, 14, 26, 51, 187–88

Washington, marijuana legalization, 226, 245

Wavy Gravy's Hog Farm, 105–6

Weather Underground, 227–28

Whatever Happened to the Hippies? (Anderson), 100

"What's After Pot?" (forum), 4, 8–15

Whitethorn, 66–67

Whitethorn Construction, 99–100

Whitethorn Junction, 66, 87

Whitethorn Post Office, 192

Whitethorn Riders, 85

Whitman, Walt, 65

Wilde, Jim, 42–43, 80–83, 209

Wilde, Mikal Xylon "Mike," 42–44, 80–82

Emma's visit in jail, 211–15

preliminary hearing of, 207–8

shooting by, 35–37, 164–67, 207–8

trial of, 208–10

Wilde, Shadrach, 81–83

William (Mare's helper), 152, 239–40

Wise, Kioma, 89

Wiyot Massacre, 64

Women's Radio Collectively (radio show), 130–38

Worldpeace, Emma, 34–46,
74–89, 126–38, 164–69,
205–15
at Berkeley, 126–29, 131–32,
165
birth of, 37–40
brother Mike's shooting
and, 35–37, 164–69,
207–15
at Chico State, 205–6
childhood of, 40–46, 74–80,
82–89
growing up in marijuana
culture, 44–46, 75–82,
130–38
jail visit to brother Mike,
211–15

marijuana legalization and,
137–38, 167, 191
mother's arrest for growing
marijuana, 77–81
return to southern Humboldt,
131–32, 206–7
"sad-ass" stories of childhood,
83–89
youth deaths in southern
Humboldt and, 85–89,
127–33, 168–69

Zavie (Crockett's coworker), 18,
21, 22, 24–25, 31–32,
107–8, 109, 189, 220, 221

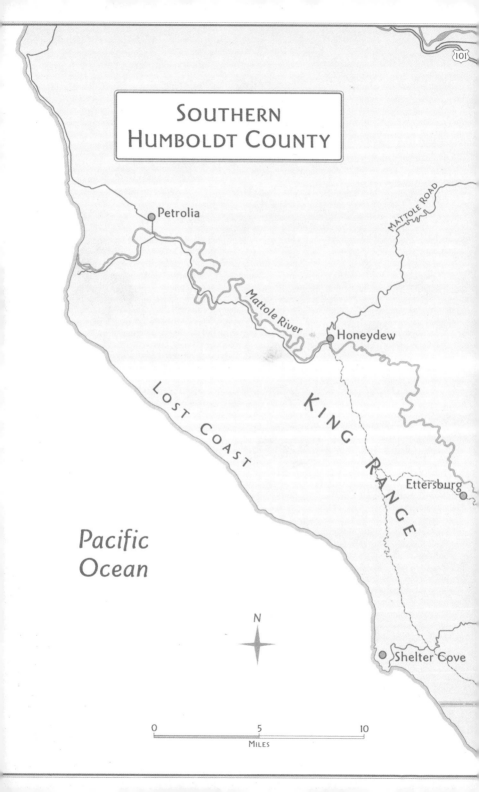